Creativity. Passion. Challe[...] the teaching ministry of Fre[...] the singles community of [...]. His new book, *The God Whisperer*, makes powerful scriptural truths accessible to everyone.

—Gene Appel, Senior Pastor, Eastside Christian Church, Fullerton, CA

In his wonderful new book *The God Whisperer*, Fred Bittner uses his canine friends to explore the simple truth that Christianity is not about going to church or following rules or accumulating points for good works. It's about the relationship you have with God. Pure and simple. One on one. In my last book I put it this way: "I thought to myself how easy it is to get so wrapped up in the task at hand, the bit of training, the trick, the discipline, that we forget about the most important part of the relationship with our horse, or anyone else, for that matter. The relationship itself. When you get that right, the rest is easy. Horses know this when they unconditionally give you their trust and their allegiance." So do dogs. And Fred's dogs illustrate in a compelling and delightful way that this is all God asks of us. Get the relationship right. This is a book you won't soon forget.

—Joe Camp, author of *The Soul of a Horse: Life Lessons from the Herd,* Creator of the canine superstar Benji

In his book *The God Whisperer,* Fred Bittner brings us to the dog world, a simple, unpretentious world of obedience, relationship, and dependence. In three well-written sections, Bittner covers most of the major struggles that folks have in their connections with God, from God as "Pack Leader," to His unswerving participation in our lives that encourages us to have intimacy, trust, and patience. Bittner not only comes at this work from the perspective of a dog lover but an obvious God lover. His stories will make you both laugh and tear-up as you identify with all that he says.

You'll appreciate his witty remarks, such as, "It seems like our wandering takes two forms. We wander for reasons, and we wander for seasons," after which Fred builds an incredible lesson that encourages the reader to "come" and rest with his Master. If you're looking for both pleasure and profundity, this Bible study will be right up your alley.

—Rick Hathaway, author *A Love Driven Life/A Legacy of Faith*

It has been my pleasure to know Fred Bittner since his college days at San Jose Bible College in the 70's. I have watched with joy his powerful Kingdom impact through youth ministry, pastor, teacher, and now creative writer. It is a joy to recommend him as a man of high Christian character who will continue to impact the world through his dynamic gift mix and dedication to touching others with God's grace and love.

—Bryce Jessup, President William Jessup University

Reading a book by Fred Bittner is like sitting down with a trusted pastor, teacher, or parent to receive excellent advice that resounds in the head and changes the heart forever. In *The God Whisperer,* this new, up-and-coming author illuminates the heart of a loving God with humor and wisdom as he gently "whispers" His truth through his word.

—Arty Vangeloof, Community Compassion Pastor, Eastside Christian Church, Fullerton, CA

the God *whisperer*

*growing in obedience
the pack leader's way*

Fred Bittner

the God *whisperer*

*growing in obedience
the pack leader's way*

TATE PUBLISHING & *Enterprises*

The God Whisperer
Copyright © 2010 by Fred Bittner. All rights reserved.

No part of this publication may be reproduced, stored in a retrieval system or transmitted in any way by any means, electronic, mechanical, photocopy, recording or otherwise without the prior permission of the author except as provided by USA copyright law.

Scripture quotations taken from the *New American Standard Bible*®, Copyright © 1960, 1962, 1963, 1968, 1971, 1972, 1973, 1975, 1977, 1995 by The Lockman Foundation. Used by permission.

This novel is a work of fiction. Names, descriptions, entities, and incidents included in the story are products of the author's imagination. Any resemblance to actual persons, events, and entities is entirely coincidental.

This novel is a work of fiction. However, several names, descriptions, entities, and incidents included in the story are based on the lives of real people.

This book is designed to provide accurate and authoritative information with regard to the subject matter covered. This information is given with the understanding that neither the author nor Tate Publishing, LLC is engaged in rendering legal, professional advice. Since the details of your situation are fact dependent, you should additionally seek the services of a competent professional.

The opinions expressed by the author are not necessarily those of Tate Publishing, LLC.

Published by Tate Publishing & Enterprises, LLC
127 E. Trade Center Terrace | Mustang, Oklahoma 73064 USA
1.888.361.9473 | www.tatepublishing.com

Tate Publishing is committed to excellence in the publishing industry. The company reflects the philosophy established by the founders, based on Psalm 68:11,
"The Lord gave the word and great was the company of those who published it."

Book design copyright © 2010 by Tate Publishing, LLC. All rights reserved.
Cover design by Amber Gulilat
Illustration by Lisa Doyle & Kim Bittner
Authors Photo by Tonya Graham
Interior design by Stefanie Rooney

Published in the United States of America

ISBN: 978-1-61566-968-4
1. Religion, Christian Life, Spiritual Growth
10.02.23

Dedication

This book is dedicated to my brothers and sisters from One in Christ. You inspired me to draw closer to God, to think of Scripture in new ways, and to become more creative as a teacher.

Thanks to the One in Christ leadership, for your unwavering support. Special thanks goes to Lisa Doyle for all your help with this project.

Thank you, Kim, for being an amazing wife. We are a dynamic team, and I could not imagine doing this work without you.

Table of Contents

Introduction *13*

SECTION ONE
Flocks, Packs, and the Church

New Perspectives on Time-Honored Lessons *21*
   The Pack Leader *25*
   The Pack Leader's Role *31*

SECTION TWO
Truth in Simple Commands

Acts of Surrender *41*
   Down—More Than a Posture *47*
   Settle—Building Intimacy with Jesus *61*

Acts of Discipleship *69*
   Sit—Choosing the Right Thing *73*
   Leave It—Yielding Authority *81*
   Take It—Trust the One Who Knows *91*

Acts of Faithfulness *99*
   Come—Your Source of Strength *103*
   Wait—Trusting God's Timing *109*
   Stay—Spiritually Strong in Tough Times *117*

SECTION THREE
Learning from the Pack

Pulling As a Team *129*
    The Power of the Pack *131*
    The Support of the Pack *137*
    The Hope of the Pack *143*

Epilogue *147*

Bibliography *155*

Introduction

Welcome to *The God Whisperer*. I am assuming that you were intrigued by the title. Maybe the picture on the cover caught your eye. Perhaps you picked up this book because you saw a movie called *The Horse Whisperer* or watched the National Geographic television show called *The Dog Whisperer* and wondered if there was any correlation. With the former, a trainer seemed to understand horses and possessed the ability to train them through a method known as whispering. In the latter, we find a trainer who understands both the dog and owner, helping to change the behavior of both.

Now that you have this book, *The God Whisperer*,

in your hand, you may be wondering what ability I am claiming. Let me answer this question before the journey even begins:

> I am not the God Whisperer. I do not claim any "special ability" to whisper on God's behalf. This book is not about me. It is, however, named for the one who does have the ability to whisper on behalf of God.

You see, Jesus came that he might show us the Father. He boldly proclaimed, "I and the Father are One" (John 10:30). He also declared, "I am the way, and the truth, and the life; no one comes to the Father, but through Me. If you had known Me, you would have known My Father also; from now on you know Him, and have seen Him" (John 14:6–7). It is Jesus who has the ability to whisper for God. He knows us, he knows the Father, and he is able to show us the way to a fulfilling spiritual life. Of Jesus, the apostle wrote,

> "And He is the image of the invisible God, the firstborn of all creation. For by Him all things were created, both in the heavens and on earth, visible and invisible, whether thrones or dominions or rulers or authorities—all things have been created by Him and for Him. And he is before all things, and in Him all things hold together."
>
> Colossians 1:15–17

He is the one who is qualified to teach us what it means to be God's children. He is the God Whisperer. This book represents the ageless message of God's love in a contemporary way so that you can experience God at a new level. It is a book about obedience. It uses contemporary illustrations from our favorite household pets as a way to apply biblical principles to our spiritual lives.

About the Author

My wife, Kim, and I own Australian terriers, a fantastic breed of dogs but often a breed that is very difficult to acquire. You will get to know them through many of the stories used in the book. We happily work with our dogs and on occasion show them at various dog shows. It is a fun hobby, but it is just that—a hobby.

I wear several other titles, ones that are more important than that of dog owner. I am first a believer in Jesus Christ. He is my Lord and Savior, and I wear His name in all of life's circumstances. I am a husband, father, and grandfather. Kim and I have been married thirty-five years, have three grown children, all married, and to date have five grandchildren (which, of course, can change anytime within nine months of the writing of this book). I am also a pastor serving as leader for One in Christ, a ministry to single adults in Southern California. I am also a professional educator. I teach middle school students in the public school. I also teach public school teachers in their credentialing programs.

The Whispering Concept Takes Shape

As a teacher, I have discovered ways of applying the whispering techniques of Cesar Millan (*The Dog Whis-*

perer) in the classroom. Let me explain what I mean. Schools have set discipline plans that include rules, boundaries, and limitations just as Cesar discusses. Schools have unique ideas built into their plans: foggers, strokes and pokes, and various other aptly named tricks to maintain a balance of leadership in the classroom. Yet I have found that young teachers walk away from their training on classroom management, having very few comprehensible solutions to their classroom dilemmas. They get the discipline plan but find it difficult to picture it happening.

"Go and purchase a year of *The Dog Whisperer*," I tell the new teachers I work with. "Watch it straight through and then come talk to me." I am usually met with puzzled looks with responses that question my advice. I'm used to that response, but I continue to encourage them to do it anyway. I know that they will hit an episode that drives a stake right through the problem they are experiencing in the classroom. They are able to see how to use the management techniques they heard about in their teacher training. They watch it happen on the screen and witness the near-instant transformation in a dog's behavior.

Through the canine illustrations, teachers are able to see themselves as leaders of their classroom. They see how setting rules, boundaries, and limitations, makes sense. They begin to apply the principles of the school discipline plan in a new way because they saw it demonstrated, not in a classroom, but with a pack of dogs. The application is very different, but the concepts are the same. One teacher working with thirty-six students doesn't make the job easy. Whispering principles, like classroom management techniques, help us to recognize and alter events, sometimes before they happen.

Invariably, the teachers who follow my advice come back saying, "I get it! I understand how to be the leader of my classroom." From there, we make huge strides together to sharpen their skills as an educator. Usually, they become hooked on the show and find their own ways to apply whispering principles. I have watched struggling teachers become excellent teachers, seemingly overnight. Many of them move on to help others understand good classroom management. I hear them direct other teachers to *The Dog Whisperer,* and I smile.

As a pastor to single-parent families, I am constantly writing new curriculum for the next series in our singles ministry. We were coming to an end of an amazing series on *The Art of Worship,* and I was seeking the Lord's input on what we should study next. One day, as I was praying through a number of ideas I had written down, the ideas for this book began to take shape. Interestingly, God whispering was not even on the list. I was struck with the idea that principles of discipleship and a solid relationship with Jesus might be more easily understood if we apply concepts of dog training here as well. It made sense, so I began to jot notes, matching ideas to Scripture. I was amazed at the way I was able to take simple principles I had learned in dog training classes and find corresponding applications in the Bible. In the end, I was amazed at the way this book came together and received confirmation from the people of One in Christ who worked through it with me.

The God Whispering Journey

This book provides a powerful way of building a relationship with Jesus. It has the potential to transform your relationship with God by bringing you back to the very basics, giving you a comprehensible and perhaps even a visual way to understand what Jesus wants to do in your life.

Take this journey with me. Invite others to do the same. Let Jesus teach you how to have a deeper relationship with the heavenly Father than you have now. Use this book as a guide for your small group or Bible school class. As others have inspired me, so I hope to inspire you. I pray that Jesus will lead you to apply this book in ways I have not even thought of myself. *The God Whisperer* will reshape your relationship with God, because the profound will be made simple through current, practical illustration.

SECTION ONE
Flocks, Packs, and the Church

New Perspectives on Time-Honored Lessons

Animals have always been a part of my life. My introduction to caring for pets came through my parents. I grew up with a dog named Tippy, a parakeet named Quarky, and a tortoise named Skipper. The dog was part of the family before I was. As the household's main pet, he ruled the backyard, and in the evening was granted access to the house. Skipper had been used in the opening of a children's shoe store. When the novelty wore off, he came home to live with us. Skipper could be found roaming the backyard, except for the months when he was hibernating. Even then, we knew where he was. Skipper dug a sizeable hole for himself under a large hedge of ivy in our backyard. Quarky, the blue parakeet lived in a cage in the corner of the kitchen. His vocabulary included a series of whistles and the words, *pretty bird,* which he learned from a bird training record my dad had purchased. Evenings were spent with my father sitting in his easy chair with Tippy at his side and Quarky perched on his shoulder. Through my father, I learned that having pets was a positive experience.

While I was in college, my father adopted a Chihuahua, which he named Snooper. He was a small dog but very noisy. He was also fiercely protective of my father. In an attempt to train Snooper, my father sought the help of a couple of dog training books. What he learned from the books became his constant joke. If Snooper jumped on him, Dad was supposed to put his knee in the dog's chest. While it could never happen with such a small dog, my father often used it as a funny threat.

Dad owned a shoe store in Pleasanton, California. It was a big job that he seemed on the surface to handle well. We did not realize until much too late that his thriving business produced more stress than he could bear alone. Unfortunately, a major heart attack took my father's life at the age of fifty-one. Our family was devastated, but the most demonstrative of the mourners was the Chihuahua. The dog spent days in the family room, protecting my father's favorite chair. He spent evenings whimpering endlessly at the loss of his master. The sides of Snooper's face seemed to have permanent stains from tears shed in the days following my father's passing.

Prior to his death, my father recorded a series of radio commercials for his store. In the days following the funeral, no one had thought to call the radio station and cancel the radio spots. After the relatives were gone and the house had grown quiet, my mother turned on the radio to break the stifling silence. Sure enough, while the radio was on, my father's voice boomed through the speaker. Snooper, jumped from my father's chair and stood before the speaker, tilting his head from side to side, waiting for my father to immerge from the radio and make all things better.

Through this experience, I learned that dogs have an acute awareness of their surroundings and the relationship they have with their master. While they live in the moment, they understand the dynamics of their pack. My father was Snooper's pack leader, and his passing left a void that the dog did not know how to fill. Deep within us is a similar void—a God-shaped void—that must be filled if we are going to live a fulfilled life.

Like Snooper, we attempt to fill the emptiness and make sense out of life. Many hope that the void can be filled by what comes out of the speakers of our radios, stereos, and televisions. We try to feel better by adding to our possessions, throwing ourselves into our jobs, or purchasing every new toy that hits the market. We attempt to convince ourselves that if we can make our lives look better than others around us, we will be fulfilled. We try to fill the pack leader's role, but at best, we can only mask the pain. There is only one who can fill the void inside of our souls. Jesus Christ is the only leader who has the ability to complete us and make our lives full. So, to use the words of the canine world, we are not complete until Jesus Christ becomes our pack leader.

The Pack Leader

The Scripture is filled with word pictures used to explain the relationship between Christ and the church. He said, "I am the bread of life" (John 6:48). He used pictures of living water and new wine. He called Himself the Alpha and Omega, and the "way, truth and life" (John 14:6). He is the vine with us being the branches (John 15:5). The church has also been explained in terms of word pictures. We are called the bride of Christ. We are described as the body of Christ. Christians are the individual parts of the body, functioning together to make one complete whole.

One of the most powerful pictures is found in John

chapter 10. Jesus said, "I am the good shepherd; the good shepherd lays down His life for the sheep... I am the good shepherd; and I know My own, and My own know Me" (John 10:11, 14). The picture of a shepherd and his sheep would be very easily understood to all those who heard these words of Jesus. Flocks of sheep lined the countryside. They had many uses, which included being used for sacrifice. When Jesus spoke about sheep, people could relate to what he was talking about.

While on staff at a Christian college in Boise, Idaho, I attended a couples' retreat in the mountains near McCall. The retreat center was well off of the two-lane highway that cut a path through the area known as Round Valley. Once off the main road, we traveled several miles up a dirt road into the hills. With me was The Image of Christ, a vocal quintet that traveled with me. The group and I were very busy in the early part of the retreat, but we needed to leave early to preach a series of meetings in a nearby town. So we packed up our van and left early on Sunday morning.

About a mile outside of the camp, we encountered a large flock of sheep. They were moving slowly down the narrow mountain road in front of us. Since there was no room for our van to pass, we were forced to follow the flock as they moved down the road. The shepherd walked in the midst of the flock. His herding dog moved around the edges, urging them to remain together. The view from our van provided an interesting discussion for my Christian college students.

We observed how the sheep remained close to their shepherd. They trusted their shepherd, though the mountainside rose steeply on the right and dropped off sharply to the left. We discussed the stories of Jesus and gained a whole new perspective on the concept of what it means to trust our Shepherd. After about a half hour of following the flock of sheep, the road widened enough that we could begin moving through the mass of wool-covered bodies.

Once we were clear of the sheep, we thought we were free of the obstruction and had learned all we were going to learn from the sheep. We were wrong. Just ahead of the flock by about a quarter of a mile, we encountered a sizable wolf. He was busy sniffing the air and hurriedly digging a hole behind a large rock. The picture was too fascinating to rush by, so we slowed to a stop, watching as the wolf dug, turned around, and backed into the hole to see if it was deep enough. When he found it wasn't deep enough, he crawled back out to continue his digging. The presence of the wolf renewed the discussion of John chapter 10—"The good shepherd lays down his life for his sheep."

The view from the mountainside is a wonderful example of the Christian life. Peter warns us, "Be of sober spirit, be on the alert. Your adversary, the devil, prowls about like a roaring lion, seeking someone to devour" (1 Peter 5:8). Around every corner—when we least expect it—Satan has dug himself into the hillside or behind a rock and is waiting for us to pass by. If we are not close to the Shepherd of our souls, listening to His voice and following His lead, then we are vulnerable to temptation and attack.

Jesus often illustrated His lessons by using images

that were around him. He used an out-of-season fig tree to teach a lesson about being ready, a well to teach about living water, and the weather to talk about faith. Many of his illustrations used sheep. People understood what He was talking about because they could see the lesson right before their eyes.

The largest portion of America's population is found in our cities, where flocks of sheep are nowhere to be found. When we do see sheep, they are in controlled environments, like a petting zoo. We may catch a glimpse of sheep on television or in the movies, but these environments are not indicative of real life. What was culturally commonplace more than 2,000 years ago as the object of His lesson is a little more difficult for us to visualize today. In our modern world, Jesus would likely use other examples to illustrate His lessons. One thing Americans do understand is the canine world. According to the 2005–2006 National Pet Owners Survey, 50 million American homes, share 73 million dogs. Many homes have multiple dogs. In addition, they also have 90 million cats. Roughly 63 million homes in America have at least one pet, making pet ownership a 40 billion dollar per year industry.

It is not a stretch, then, to gain a new perspective of the deep spiritual lessons of Jesus by applying what He said about sheep and about discipleship to what we know about dogs and obedience. Jesus is our pack leader. He is the Lord and Master to all who claim His name. The following chapters will take the timeless lessons of Jesus and illustrate them by looking at the simple commands we use with our dogs.

Think It Through

Passages used to illustrate "The Pack Leader": John 15:5; John 6:48; John 10:11 and 14; 1 Peter 5:8

John 15:5 — I am the vine you are the branches.
If a man remains in me and I in him
he will bear much fruit
apart from me you can do nothing

John 6:48 — I am the bread of life.

John 10:11 — I am the good shepherd.
The good shepherd lays down his life for the sheep.

14:1 — Trust in God; trust also in me.

1 Peter 5:8 — Your enemy the devil prowls around...

The Pack Leader's Role

My first introduction to the social interactions of the pack came from the pen of Jack London and his book, *The Call of the Wild*. This book about dog sledding across the state of Alaska has become a classic among young readers. The book has been analyzed by critics, interpreted by sociologists, and evaluated by outdoorsmen. At one point, I read a critique by a Christian writer who believed that *The Call of the Wild* was evolutionary propaganda. I read another interpretation that the end of the book proved that London was pushing the concept of reincarnation. London's daughter spoke of a time when her dad was questioned about the interpretations placed upon his book. He was puzzled by what others saw in his writing, so he decided to reread his own book several times in an attempt to figure out why there were so many wild interpretations. In the end, he confessed that he did not know what all of the fuss was about. It was just a book about dogs, their master, and a race across Alaska.

The Call of the Wild is a story about a dog named Buck, who is taken from his home in Santa Clara, California, shipped to Alaska by way of the black market, and sold as a sled dog during the Alaskan gold rush. It chronicles the lessons that Buck learns in his new Alaskan environment and his eventual rise to leader of his pack. The story paints a very clear lesson of a natural chain of command, where the master creates the vision. The pack leader has the closest relationship to the master and is the most responsive to his desires. The pack leader then communicates the master's instruction to the rest of the pack.

In the animal world, there is no more important role than that of pack leader; whether it is the animals of the jungle, a team of dogs in Alaska, or the dogs in your backyard. The group must have a clear understanding of who is in charge and the role that each member in the group must fulfill. There is security in knowing how each of the members fit into their social environment. When the dominant leader disappears, the whole hierarchy of the pack is upset, leaving new potential leaders to compete for control. This concept is true with humans as well.

When a business leader becomes weak, or is not

viewed as able to take the group to the next level, power struggles ensue until a new leader takes over the position. When that happens, the business begins to act differently, according to the temperament of that new leader. This is true whether the leadership is a positive or a negative one. However, over time (sometimes very little time), the organization will rebel against the negative leader. This person will not remain in leadership very long because angry, demanding, "my way or the highway" leadership is ultimately viewed as weak. What people, churches, and businesses need is positive, confident leadership that communicates a sense of purpose.

Cesar Millan, noted dog expert, applies this idea to the dog world. He believes that calm-assertive leadership is what is necessary for a healthy pack. The pack leader takes on the responsibility for the life, the social relationships, and the overall health of the pack. It is the pack leader who brings the pack to food and water. It is the pack leader who settles disputes, decides when the pack moves, and when it rests. In other words, the pack leader sets all of the rules that the pack must live by. Millan says, "Pack leaders are clearly very confident dogs, and it comes naturally to them. They aren't faking it, and they couldn't if they tried" (*Cesar's Way* 115).

Jesus conquered sin and death. He became a man, suffered all of the pain that we experience, died our death on the cross, and rose again. As a result, Jesus could clearly say, "All authority has been given to Me in heaven and on earth" (Matthew 28:18). As the Apostle Paul stated, "He made him who knew no sin to be sin on our behalf, that we might become the righteousness of God in Him" (2 Corinthians 5:21).

> Jesus is Lord. He is not faking it. He couldn't if He tried. His disciples, the early church, and 2,000 years of Christians would have figured it out.

If you have come face-to-face with the lordship of Jesus Christ and have accepted him as your Savior, then he must become your leader as well. Paul writes, "Or do you not know that your body is a temple of the Holy Spirit who is in you, whom you have from God, and that you are not your own? For you have been bought with a price; therefore, glorify God in your body" (1 Corinthians 6:19–20). Jesus asked an important question regarding this issue, "And why do you call Me, Lord, Lord, and do not do what I say?" (Luke 6:46).

I had an amazing discussion with a ten-year-old girl who was considering giving her life over to the lordship of Christ. She had come to our church with a friend and was interested in knowing more about becoming a Christian. We had spent quite a bit of time looking in the Scripture, talking about what it meant to accept Jesus, when she stopped me with a question: "You mean that if I accept Jesus as my lord, then I will have a grown up living inside of me, and I will have to do what He says?" I had never heard it stated so profoundly, and by a child nonetheless. I assured her that she was very insightful and completely correct.

In the end, she decided that she was not ready to make that much of a commitment. She wasn't sure that she could completely turn her life over to a grownup like Jesus. She acknowledged that he was Lord. She was also convinced that she wanted to follow him eventually, but she would not make such a commitment unless she could do so with 100 percent dedication. She finished by explaining that her mom had taught her that she should never do anything halfway.

Like the ten-year-old girl in my office, I don't want to do things halfway. God's way is never halfway. I need to trust him 100 percent, yield to him as the Lord of my life, accept his vision for me, and follow his plan. Because of this desire, I have come to learn that living in the center of God's will leads to a balanced, fulfilled life.

I have some friends who had a pet parakeet. This was not just any parakeet. He was a very beloved bird. He had the run (or the fly) of the house. You might have found him in the bathroom chatting with his friend in the mirror or in the master bedroom visiting with the friend that was in that mirror. Or, he would be in the living room playing with the decorations on the tables (which were probably more for him than for decoration). When Walt was home, however, you would find the bird perched on his hand, kissing his ring, or sitting on Jean's shoulder. It was clear to anyone who visited their home that the parakeet adored his owners.

One day, Walt made the mistake he always dreaded. He walked out onto his front porch with the bird still perched on his shoulder. Almost instantly, the bird saw his opportunity to give his wings a true test. He rose from Walt's shoulder and flew in a straight line away from his master. The frantic couple called out to their bird, but he was rapidly disappearing from sight. Then it seemed like the bird realized that being away from the people he loved was not freedom at all, but bondage.

Suddenly he made a sweeping left turn and began to make his way back in the direction of the house. For a time, the bird was not visible and seemed lost. As if from nowhere, the bird swept over the roof of the house and landed on his master's shoulder. Freedom may look exciting, but the promise of life with a master who loves you and has a plan for your life is much greater. <u>Like the father who watched and waited for his prodigal son to return, our God is waiting for us to come full circle and return to him.</u> Perhaps this is what Peter meant when he said, "Repent and return" (Acts 3:19). When we realize the value of being a child of God, we return to him willingly, wanting nothing more than to dwell in his presence.

Think It Through

Passages used to illustrate "The Pack Leader's Role": Matthew 28:18; 2 Corinthians 5:21; 1 Corinthians 6:19–20; Luke 6:46; Acts 3:19

On Your Own

Can you say with confidence that Jesus is your pack leader? Identify three things that you do regularly that demonstrate your relationship with God.

_____

_____

_____

The God Whisperer

The pack leader takes on the responsibility for the life, the social relationships, and the overall health of the pack. Are you following his lead or running on ahead? Write down one area in your life where you are waiting on the Lord's leading.

___

The Sermon on the Mount gives a number of insights into those who accept the pack leader's role. Read through the sermon, found in Matthew chapters 5–7. As you read, ask the Lord to help you set five spiritual growth goals.

___

All authority has been given me M 28:18

He made Him who knew no sin to be sin on our behalf. 2 Cor 5:21

Why do you call Me, Lord and do not do what I say. L. 6:46.

Repent and Return. A. 3:19.

SECTION TWO
Truth in Simple Commands

Acts of Surrender

When you watch a dog show on the television, you are generally exposed to what happens in the best in show ring. In these competitions, dogs are judged against the standard of their breed. The dog that comes closest to that standard on a given day is awarded the prize. The best specimen in each breed moves to the group competition, where they are judged against other winners in their group (terriers, hounds, working, sporting, non sporting, herding, and toy). When an animal is deemed best in the group, they are moved to the best in show competition. It is a lively spectacle, with large audiences all screaming for the representative in their own group to win.

While all of the excitement is going on in the main ring, there is another competition taking place, usually off in one corner of the field. This competition does not judge against a breed standard but against the level of obedience shown to the master. There are rarely large crowds, public address systems, or announcers. This arena is very quiet. In fact, very few words are spoken. Commands are simple: "heel" or "sit"; "down" or "come." Dogs are expected to watch the master at all times. They read their face, sense the flexing of their muscles, and respond to the smallest movement of the hand. They must be so sensitive to their master that they can respond from across the ring, while their master's back is turned.

According to the American Kennel Club, teams in "the Novice Class demonstrate good canine companion skills such as heeling, both with and without a leash, coming when called, standing for a simple physical examination, and staying in both a sit and a down position with a group of dogs." Once these skills are mastered, the team moves to open class and then the utility class. With each level, new and more difficult skills are added such as retrieving and scent discrimination. The ultimate goal for the obedience team is being awarded the Obedience Trial Championship (OTCH) title. This title is often called the "PhD" for dogs, and is the highest obedience honor a dog can receive. At the top obedience levels, dogs are expected to be able to work by hand signals alone. The goal of the obedience competition is to demonstrate the dog's ability to "act as one" with their master.

Jesus used similar wording to describe his relationship with the heavenly Father. "I and the Father are one" (John 10:30). In those six words, Jesus described both his equality and his level of intimacy with God. They were one in power and authority, but they were also one in mind and heart.

Using those words to describe his level of intimate knowledge of the Father angered the religious leaders of his time. To describe himself as one with the Father would mean that he had a relationship that was beyond equal. How could this Jesus know more than those who had dedicated their lives to wear the priestly robes? How could he claim more authority that those of the Jewish leaders? What qualified him to claim such knowledge? Could anyone have that kind of a relationship with God the Father?

The good news of the gospel is that Jesus had that relationship, and through him we gain special access to the Father. Through Jesus, we come to understand the wisdom and the heart of God. However, a relationship with the Father is not achieved by memorizing Bible verses. Nor is it achieved by putting in seat time at church. While each is important in building our relationship with God, memorization and seat time are not proof of a relationship with the living God. A relationship with God is one we must experience ourselves.

Near the end of his ministry, Jesus offered a very powerful prayer to the Father. The gospels rarely describe the details of his prayers, but this particular prayer is reported word for word.

> "Sanctify them in truth. Thy word is truth. As Thou didst send Me into the world, I also have sent them into the world. And for their sakes I sanctify Myself, that they themselves also may be sanctified in truth. I do not ask on behalf of these alone, but for those also who believe in Me through their word; that they may all be one; even as Thou, Father, art in Me, and I in Thee, that they also may be in Us; that the world may believe that Thou didst send Me."
>
> John 17:17–21

Imagine the reality of this prayer. Jesus was praying for his disciples, but he was looking beyond them to those who would believe the gospel. He was praying for you. The goal of his prayer was that you might be set apart today for an everlasting relationship with God. Developing the kind of relationship that Jesus described in his prayer takes time. It requires more than a cursory look at the Scriptures on Sunday. Claiming such a relationship of harmony with God demands that you allow Him access to every part of your life to shape and mold to His will. It requires that you "present your bodies a living and holy sacrifice, acceptable to God, which is your spiritual service of worship" (Romans 12:1).

In this section, called "Acts of Surrender," we join the novice class of spiritual obedience. Like the animals in the novice class, we must demonstrate mastery of the basic commands of Jesus before we are able to move toward the higher disciplines. These commands are the foundation that leads to spiritual maturity. Getting to this level involves a time commitment, lots of practice, and plenty of patience. In canine obedience, dog and master must be of one mind working together as a unit, with the dog responsive to the slightest command of the master. Obedience to Christ is much the same way.

Instant spiritual maturity does not exist. We must start with the simple commands of Christ, and grow from there. "Down" and "Settle" are two postures we must take in order to develop the kind of relationship that Jesus described. These principles help lay the framework for growing in knowledge, understanding, and wisdom. If Jesus said that we could be one with Him and the Father, shouldn't we do our part so that we may receive the blessings that God has planned for us?

Think It Through

Passages used to illustrate the introduction to "Acts of Surrender": John 10:30; John 17:17–21; Romans 12:1

John 10:30 — I and the Father are one.

John 17 — Thou, Father, art in Me, and I in Thee.

they also may be in Us, that the world may believe that Thou didst send Me.

Romans 12:1

DOWN
More Than a Posture

Kim and I specialize in a breed of dogs called Australian terriers. Jazzy, our female Aussie, is a classic black and tan, and is an AKC champion in conformation shows. She is also a very high-energy pet. She can run circles around dogs much larger than herself and jumps with ease over the three-foot exercise pens that we have erected for her safety. She has also been known to leap six feet from chair to chair in the living room from a standing position. Satchmo is our red male. He is younger than Jazzy and is just getting started in the conformation process. He is larger and has a much more laid-back disposition. He is very content to spend his evenings stretched out on the floor at Kim's feet while Jazzy bounces from location to location.

We were delighted when the local community center offered a beginning agility class and a beginning obedience class during the same time period. We could be outside with the dogs, and we could all get some exercise. Jazzy and I signed up for agility, while Kim accompanied Satchmo to the obedience class.

Agility class took place on a large, elevated lawn next to the community center. I quickly discovered that agility is a good workout for both owner and animal. Dogs get to run through tunnels and hoops, over teeter-totters and jumps, all for speed and accuracy. Owners just get to run (and make happy comments to encourage their dogs). Jazzy thoroughly enjoyed the class. She insisting on going over the jumps set up for the bigger dogs and shunned the jumps designated for the smaller dogs. Her favorite part of the course seemed to be the A frame, which is a long ramp that's hinged in the middle. Dogs are supposed to run up one side and down the other while giving their best impression of Rin Tin Tin. The final test before graduation from agility class was a timed trial through the entire course. Jazzy finished second in her class of thirty dogs, only because I fell in the middle of the course, and she had to stop and wait for me.

Satchmo's beginning obedience class was located

in the parking lot below the grassy field. This class was designed to teach basic obedience commands allowing dog and owner to work together. The gruff-voiced instructor worked with a dozen or so eager pets and owners. There were no jumps or hoops, no races or times, just periods of sitting, walking on a lead, and the all-important *down* position. On the final day of our classes, the gruff-voiced man was testing both owners and dogs to make sure that they were worthy of the photocopied certificate he had prepared ahead of time. The final portion of the test was a three-minute sustained down. This meant that each dog was to remain in a down position with a loose lead, on the left side of their owner. The group was halfway through the down portion of the test as Jazzy and I were taking our last practice run on the agility course. For the final agility test, the instructor had raised the A frame to a little over six feet high. From this height, Jazzy could easily see over a row of parked cars to the group of dogs, all in their down position awaiting their next command. Kim and Satchmo were in the middle of that group.

At the pinnacle of the A frame, Jazzy noticed Kim and Satchmo who were doing something in the parking lot that did not involve her. Apparently, this was unacceptable, because Jazzy took a flying leap off of the top of the A frame, jerking the lead out of my hand and leaving me fighting to maintain my balance. At a dead run, Jazzy crossed the field, made her way down the hill, through the parking lot, and into the middle of the group of quiet dogs. What followed was nothing short of complete mayhem. Dogs abandoned their test, rose to their feet, and started jumping and barking. Frustrated owners tried to control their animals while the unsettled instructor gasped and sputtered commands in an attempt to regain control of his class. After all, the purpose of the three-minute drill was a test to show that the dogs could close out all distractions for a set period of time and focus their attention on their master. Jazzy had become the distraction that caused every dog to lose focus and fail the test.

Down, as an act of submission, is a difficult challenge for a dog. Although we deal only with domesticated dogs, they still react to genetics. In the wild, lying down means that a dog is yielding authority to the dominant dog of the pack. Assuming that position means the dominant one is allowed to stand over them.

There are two forms of the down position. The difference is very subtle, but the effect on the dog is very dramatic. For the sake of any better terms, I will refer to them as *basic down* and *advanced down*. Dogs assume both the basic and advanced down naturally, depending on their own mood, but to assume these positions on command is not a natural thing. Most owners teach only the basic down position.

The basic down position begins with sit and drops from there with front legs forward and back legs in a sort of a crouched position. To teach this position, show the dog a treat and have them sit. Then move the treat away from the dog and down toward the floor. The body will follow the nose in pursuit of the treat. Basic down is a surrender position because it allows the master to assume a higher position. However, it is still an active position since the dog is able to maintain a tense readiness. With the back legs in a crouched position, they remain ready to spring into action at the first sign of difficulty. What we want in this act of surrender is that our dog willingly gives control over to the master. As the level of trust grows deeper, the dog will relax, altering his own position by putting his or her head down on the ground as well. This level of submission is often accompanied by a heavy sigh as the dog relaxes.

The advanced down position is taught in upper-level obedience classes. As we develop a deeper level of trust with our dog, we can alter the way in which our dogs go down. In the advanced form of down, we teach the dog to rotate their hips so that both hind legs are on the same side of the body. This position increases the pet's feeling of submission and strengthens the role of the leader. In the advanced down position, a dog gives up the ability to react with quickness. Because of this, the dog must willingly yield the power to their master. This down has a deeper level of dependence and trust.

Down seems to require a willful act on behalf of our dogs. Out of the four puppies that are in our home, three (Basie, Duke, and Major) are submissive. If you put them into a down position, those three will automatically roll over. The fourth puppy (whose name is Shimmy) is the dominant dog in the litter. He finds it extremely difficult to accept down. He struggles with *sit* if he thinks that down may follow. When the down command is issued, he would rather escape.

Most of us are like Shimmy. We struggle with the idea of giving up control of our lives, yielding authority to another. We are often willing to accept Jesus as our Savior (saving us from our sin), but we are not so willing to making him our Lord (Master of our lives). Yet our ability to assume the down position is essential to building a trusting relationship with Jesus. Notice what the Psalmist had to say about down.

> "The Lord sustains all who fall and raises up all who are bowed down. The eyes of all look to Thee, and Thou dost give them their food in due time. Thou dost open Thy hand, and dost satisfy the desire of every living thing."
>
> Psalm 145:14–16

In the psalm, we can view the terms fall, bow down, and look to Thee, as poetic ways of expressing one concept. Take them together, and you have a picture of what the down position means. When we do these things, God responds by raising us up, providing for our physical needs, and fulfilling our emotional needs.

David wrote, "The Lord is my shepherd, I shall not want. He makes me lie down in green pastures" (Psalm 23:1–2a). David knew who his leader was. He knew that God was in charge.

> It did not matter if he was living through times of green pastures and still waters, or he was walking through the valley of the shadow of death. David had confidence that God was looking out for his best interest. He willingly gave up the authority of his life to the shepherd of his soul.

As a result, God led him into pastures filled with the fresh shoots of new grass.

"He makes me to lie down." To use those three words *He makes me* does not imply that we are forced into that position. It is instead a call to voluntary submission that comes naturally to those who experience the loving hand of the good Shepherd. Even though it is not forced, down does require focus. Puppies have a difficult time with focus. They are naturally curious and have a very short attention span. They are interested in every new thing that they see. They want to get into the middle of everything. They are without understanding as to what will bring them pain and what will bring them pleasure. In the midst of so many new things to smell, see, and chew on, down is a very difficult challenge.

To be successful with the down position, a master must have a purpose, a vision for what the end result will be, and sometimes the tenacity to outlast their puppy's strong will. The master must make the puppy assume the down position and then reward the results. A treat starts out to be their reward. As time goes on, however, the reward becomes the bond of trust and the deepening relationship between the owner and dog. Down becomes a positive experience. David understood God's authority and was submissive to the call to lie down. He viewed it as a very positive experience in his relationship with God.

Are you like David? Or are you more like a puppy? When we acquire a new possession, move to a new environment, get a new job, or maybe develop a new relationship, our attention is drawn away from the good Shepherd and onto that new interest. There are so many things to explore. During these times, we live out the truth of the great childhood memory verse, "All we like sheep have gone astray; we have turned every one to his own way; and the LORD hath laid on him the iniquity of us all." This Isaiah 53:6 passage is from the King James Version. I memorized it in Sunday school as a child. It is when we walk away, chasing after some new adventure, that God needs to bring us back to Himself. By accepting God's command, David experienced a world of blessings.

Like David, we want the blessings of green pastures and the refreshment of the still waters, but to receive them we must be willing to lie down before him. When we draw close to him in the good times, we gain confidence that he will also lead us through the valleys. The invitation is ours to sit at God's banqueting table. His goodness and mercies are ours for the taking. God makes each of these promises available to us, but we cannot reserve the right to turn to our own way when things get hard. Nor can we demand blessings if we are not willing to assume the position before him. We lose the joy of obedience to the Lord when we do not accept his call to submission.

Do you feel like you constantly have to learn the same lesson? Does it feel like driving around the same block over and over without finding your destination? If you feel that way, then you need to know that you are not unique. We all have "gone astray" moments (sometimes gone astray weeks, months, or years).

Though it feels as though we are on an endless loop of struggling with the same issues, we can grow through them and come to the place where a relationship with the Lord is what we desire most. The New Testament gives us a few valuable insights to help us experience green pastures and still waters.

First, we must recognize the lordship of Jesus Christ (John 10:11). Jesus is the good Shepherd. He is not *a* shepherd, but *the* Shepherd. There is no other shepherd like him. About himself, Jesus said,

> "My sheep hear My voice, and I know them, and they follow Me; and I give eternal life to them, and they shall never perish; and no one shall snatch them out of My hand. My Father, who has given them to Me, is greater than all; and no one is able to snatch them out of the Father's hand. I and the Father are one."
>
> John 10:27–30

While in Christian college, one of my professors said something that has never left me: "Leaders only lead with the consent of the led." This statement is true for any organization, but it is especially true in volunteer organizations. A leader must have a vision that people understand, have the ability to communicate that vision, formulate a plan to accomplish the vision, and rally members to bring the vision to fulfillment. However, a leader must be surrounded by people who trust the plan and accept his or her leadership.

When we recognize the lordship of Jesus and believe that there is indeed no other shepherd, we listen to his voice and follow his teaching. Listening and following can only be accomplished when we begin to practice the teaching found in 1 Peter 5:6. "Humble yourselves, therefore, under the mighty hand of God, that He may exalt you at the proper time." Humbling ourselves is a concept firmly rooted in the concept of "down."

Second, we need to trust His lordship. When we trust Jesus, we know that he will meet our needs. The writer of Proverbs gives us a picture of the results of trusting Jesus. "Then you will walk in your way securely, and your foot will not stumble. When you lie down, you will not be afraid; when you lie down your sleep will be sweet" (Proverbs 3:23–24). Paul also understood God's blessing. To his spiritual son, Timothy, Paul wrote, "For this reason I also suffer these things, but I am not ashamed; for I know whom I have believed and I am convinced that He is able to guard what I have entrusted to Him until that day" (2 Timothy 1:12). His response to that blessing is recorded in Ephesians 3:20–21: "Now to Him who is able to do exceeding abundantly beyond all that we ask or think according to the power that works within us, to Him be the glory in the church and in Christ Jesus to all generations forever and ever. Amen."

Dogs cannot fake trust. They either accept your authority or they don't. They have no concept of political correctness, and they have no interest in making believe that they trust you when they don't. You know where you stand with them. Humans, on the other hand, are very capable of putting on the show. We can follow the right steps and fit in very well. But God sees the heart. He is not fooled by hollow acts of submission. We must begin by accepting his leadership, his power, and his majesty. Then we must trust that power enough to believe that God is capable of blessing our lives under any circumstance.

Do you want to "walk in your way securely," as promised in the proverb? That level of confidence depends on our ability to come before the Lord and assume the down position. Begin with the basic down position. God will meet you in that place. He will work with you and reveal himself to you so that you can grow in your ability to trust. Eventually, you will find yourself moving to the advanced down, wanting to spend more and more quality time with God.

Think It Through

Passages used to illustrate "down": Psalm 145:14–16; Psalm 23:1–2a; Isaiah 53:6; John 10:11; John 10:27–30; 1 Peter 5:6; Proverbs 3:23–24; 2 Timothy 1:12; Ephesians 3:20–21

On Your Own

A study of James 4 gives three ingredients to success in the "down" position.

"Submit therefore to God. Resist the devil, and he will flee from you." The first act of down, as we identified above, is to recognize the lordship of Jesus Christ in your life. To submit to one and resist the other indicates that a clear choice must be made. We cannot be half of a Christian, accepting the benefits and rejecting everything else. Consider your own life. Have you submitted every part of your life to Jesus? Submitting to God is not a one-time event but a process of growth in our relationship with him. In the space below, pick one area of resistance that you would like to surrender to the Lord.

_____

_____

_____

"Draw near to God, and He will draw near to you." The second aspect of down, as described here, is to turn our entire focus onto Jesus. We draw near that he may draw near to us and speak to us as the Lord of our lives. Drawing near means that we open ourselves to examination by the Holy Spirit, who is able to teach us in the ways we should go. 1 John 5:7 says, "And it is the spirit who bears witness, because the Spirit is the truth."

Write a prayer of surrender in the section below. Ask God to draw near to you as you begin to yield this area of resistance to his control.

_____

_____

_____

"Humble yourselves in the presence of the Lord, and He will exalt you." The third aspect James identifies is the need to accept the conviction from the Holy Spirit and not turn away. Romans 8:16–17 says, "The Spirit Himself bears witness with our spirit that we are children of God. And if children, heirs also, heirs of God and fellow heirs with Christ, if indeed we suffer with Him in order that we may also be glorified with Him."

_____

_____

_____

Before moving on, think about your own quiet times. Does your prayer life seem more like the basic down or the advanced down? If you struggle to maintain focus because your mind is racing ahead to things you have to do, or you are stressing about your responsibilities, then you may be in the basic down position. You are down for sure, but you are ready to spring into action. Is God calling you to a deeper level of obedience? This will not happen until you make the decision that you are going to the advanced down. It is time to rotate the hips and give up control. Make your quiet time a genuine act of surrender by assuming the advanced down position. This is what believers mean when they speak of "practicing the presence" of God. You will find a whole new level of freedom when you assume the advanced down position. Allow God to take you into the green pastures and the still waters. Decide that you will dwell there. Yield your agenda to his will and allow him to have complete control. Humble yourself before the Lord so that he can exalt you. Look to God and let him satisfy the desires of your heart.

Now that you have looked at James 4, pray through the passage and ask God to open your eyes to areas you need to surrender.

God opposes the proud but gives grace to the humble. James 4:v & Prov. 3:3

J. 4:7 Submit yourselves to God.
Resist the devil, and he will flee from you
✱ Come near to God and he will come near to you.

SETTLE
Building Intimacy with Jesus

There are many reasons why a family would choose to adopt a pet. Quite often the reason helps to determine the kind of pet a family adopts. A goldfish won't provide much protection from an intruder, but it will provide interest to a room environment. A bird will not go outside and play fetch; that job is better left for a dog. No matter what purpose we have in mind when we adopt a pet, the ultimate need remains the same.

We adopt dogs to become a part of our family. If

your dog could speak a human language, they would tell you that they want to be a part of your family as well (although they would likely use the word *pack*). There is security in knowing you belong and are accepted. Yet this sense of belonging is often the most difficult feeling to attain. We struggle with our own insecurities and find it difficult to trust those who enter our emotional space.

Once a dog has the confidence of down, they are ready for the next step of submission—settle. Settling is a requirement of a good relationship between dog and master. It requires time, focus, and patience. Shut off the television, ignore the phone, get down on the floor, and just be still. We want our dog to be comfortable in our environment. To accomplish this, they must feel comfortable with us in their environment. The essential idea is to demonstrate that you own both environments. When they accept your mastery, then they can become comfortable with their role in either environment. They learn to trust completely.

A settled dog will not only lie down in your presence but will roll over, exposing the most vulnerable part of his or her body—the underside. Every other part of the canine body is structured for protection. Muscles and bones work together to create a very solid frame around the essential parts of the dog. The one part that is dangerously exposed is the underside below the rib cage. A truly settled dog will willingly roll over and expose their underside. It is their way of saying, "I trust you completely." That is a settled dog.

God invites us to be comfortable in his environment. He also wants us to be comfortable with him in our environment. Jesus came to earth (God with us—Emmanuel) to show us that he was Lord of both environments. For this reason, he calls us to settle before him. By letting Jesus be master in our space, we have confidence that we will reside in his. For us to settle is to expose the most vulnerable part of our lives before our God.

The writer of Hebrews urges us to settle.

> "There remains therefore a Sabbath rest for the people of God. For the one who has entered His rest has himself also rested from his works, as God did from His. Let us therefore be diligent to enter that rest, lest anyone fall through the same example of disobedience. For the word of God is living and active and sharper than any two-edged sword, and piercing as far as the division of soul and spirit, of both joints and marrow, and able to judge the thoughts and intentions of the heart. And there is no creature hidden from His sight, but all things are open and laid bare to the eyes of Him whom we have to do."
>
> Hebrews 4:10–13

Through Nathan, the prophet, God grabbed David by the back of the neck, laid him down, and exposed his disobedience. The two-edged sword pierced deeply, bringing conviction and submission.

> "I know my transgressions, and my sin is ever before me. Against Thee, Thee only, I have sinned, and done what is evil in Thy sight, So that Thou are justified when Thou dost speak, and blameless when Thou dost judge."

Psalm 51:3–4

Through his conviction, David began to pray. Verses 5–17 of Psalm 51 show how David went from being exposed by God to being settled before Him. He prayed that God would make him whiter than snow, that even the areas of life that were broken might bring rejoicing before the Lord. "Create in me a clean heart, O God, and renew a steadfast spirit in me ... the sacrifices of God are a broken spirit; A broken and a contrite heart, O God, you will not despise" (Psalm 51:10,17).

God invited us to be comfortable in his environment, but he also wanted us to be comfortable with him in our environment. So Jesus came to earth (God with us) to show that he not only owned heaven, but he was Lord on earth as well. Both environments belong to him.

Do you trust God with your greatest weakness? Psalm 46:10 says, "Be still and know that I am God." The New American Standard version says, "Cease your striving." What are the things that we strive for? Where is your focus? Is it on your job, possessions, money, or securing a retirement? God says, stop your striving. Be still. Trust me, and let me be God.

I was once invited to a church in eastern Washington to preach a revival. The building sat up on the crest of a hill. The downhill side of the auditorium was solid windows that looked out at hundreds of acres of crops, swaying in the breeze. During the hour-long service, dark clouds rolled in, the winds rose sharply, and the temperature dropped dramatically. The service was nearly over. I was singing a song based on Psalm 46, when the heavens opened with the most dramatic hailstorm I have ever experienced. I was singing, "I need to be still, and let God love me," while anxious farmers watched out the windows. Before their eyes, the storm was destroying their hard work. By the time the service concluded, very few of the crops were still standing. Everything they had strived for over the last several months was wiped out. Yet in the midst of disaster, God was saying, "Be still. Life is tough, but stop your striving." As I finished the song, I was moved to pray. What followed felt like the collective sigh of every person in the room. God was truly moving that evening. It became very clear to all that he was still in charge. He was in that place, and he was going to meet their needs.

<u>God wants to meet your needs and prove his love for you in the midst of your struggle.</u> Open your life to him. <u>Be vulnerable in his presence.</u> <u>Once you trust, you will certainly be able to obey.</u> There are times when we wander. We are not able to settle before the Lord. Yet God knows what we need, and he is very willing to help us in the settling process.

At the end of the summer this past year, our pack of Australian terriers increased to six because Jazzy gave birth to four puppies. Overnight, our living room was transformed into a puppy nursery with cute little balls of fur averaging five ounces each. Jazzy was a terrific mother, spending nearly all of her time in the whelping pen, tending to her babies. We were amazed at how Jazzy was transformed into a caring, protective, tireless mother.

As the puppies grew and began to assert their own wills, Jazzy altered her leadership over them. In order to keep them all under control, Jazzy needed to transform from a nurturing mother to that of pack leader. In his book, *Cesar's Way*, Cesar Millan explains the role of the dominant dog. The pack leader, he explains, "must present calm, assertive energy." The leader usually has a high level of energy. They are naturally confident dogs. Those who follow exhibit what he calls "calm, submissive" behavior. "They walk with their heads down, in line with their bodies, and they stay behind the pack leader while traveling, their ears relaxed or back, their tails wagging but always kept low. If the pack leader challenges them they might back away, bend down, or even lie down and roll over, exposing their bellies. By doing that, basically they're saying, 'You're the boss, and I'm not questioning that. Whatever you say goes'" (*Cesar's Way*, pp. 115–116).

Mothers will testify that young children have more energy than they know what to do with. They also have a higher level of curiosity. Everything they see becomes a new adventure. The four puppies were no exception. They needed to be trained to follow their mother's directions. Jazzy would nudge, growl, and stand in the way of her active puppies. That seemed to work for a while, but soon the group was far too active. To remain the leader of her pack, Jazzy needed to change her tactics again. When they didn't listen, she would gently bite them on the back of the neck and roll them over on their side. They would struggle, scream, and make every attempt to rebel, but Jazzy would maintain her hold until they relaxed and settled. Once they submitted to her leadership, Jazzy would release her grip and stand over the puppy to make sure that he did not move until she gave him permission. When she was confident that they had indeed settled, she would move away, allowing them to get up on their own.

Proverbs 3:12 says, "For whom the Lord loves He reproves, even as a father, the son in whom he delights." Isn't it interesting that we view discipline as negative, while God considers it as positive. The idea that God is exerting his authority over us, laying us on our side and exposing our weaknesses, can be a very frightening thing. Yet God's purpose is not to hurt us but to cause us to grow. To that end, the writer of Hebrews says, "My son, do not regard lightly the discipline of the Lord, nor faint when you are reproved by Him; For those whom the Lord loves He disciplines, and He scourges every son whom He receives" (Hebrews 12:5–6).

Whether we willingly settle before the Lord or are settled by the Lord, the end result is a new level of intimacy with our Lord Jesus Christ.

Think It Through

Passages used to illustrate "Settle": Hebrews 4:10–13; Psalm 51:3–17; Psalm 46:10; Proverbs 3:12; Hebrews 12:5–6

On Your Own

Read all of David's prayer in Psalm 51. What was at the heart of his prayer? What did he discover through his experience? What assurances did he end up with?

He cries out for God to be with him. He acknowledges his sin. He asks for restoration. The sacrifices of God are a broken spirit; a broken and contrite heart.

Is God trying to get hold of you? How can you turn that situation into a time where you settle before him?

Read Hebrews 12:5–13. Invest some time with the Lord and settle.

v 9 "... How much more should we submit to the Father of our spirits and live!"

Note: Number 6:24 "The Lord bless you and keep you, the Lord make his face shine upon you and be gracious to you, the Lord turn his face towards you and give you peace."

Acts of Discipleship

When Kim and I decided we would start taking our first Australian terrier to dog shows, we looked for a training program to help Jazzy and I learn the ropes of conformation. Fortunately, a training center was located a half mile from our house. Every Thursday night, the instructor taught several dogs and their masters how to walk in appropriate patterns. He taught us about stacking (the perfect stance based on the breed standard), walking, and presenting the best parts of our dogs to a judge. Class was fun. We learned the basics of the confirmation process, but the hard work of becoming a team in the ring took place when we were at home. Every night, Jazzy and I spent time practicing, developing our skills, and gaining confidence with each other. Without the time spent together in the quietness of our home, we would have had little success in the show arena.

The process reminded me of the concept of discipleship.

Each week, the church gathers together to learn about serving Jesus. We meet with other believers to learn the principles of our walk with Jesus. Yet, the real work of becoming a disciple of Jesus is accomplished throughout the week, where we practice our faith in our own personal quiet time.

Discipleship is a key component in the Christian faith. Without it, the church is just one generation from extinction. Paul wrote to Timothy about the importance of discipleship.

> "You therefore, my son, be strong in the grace that is in Christ Jesus. And the things which you have heard from me, in the presence of many witnesses, these entrust to faithful men, who will be able to teach others also."
>
> 2 Timothy 2:1–2

It was God's plan that the message of Jesus be spread through the church. Yet discipleship goes much deeper than what we learn on Sunday or in a Bible study.

Jesus said, "For whoever does the will of God, he is My brother and sister and mother" (Mark 3:35). To develop this level of understanding, we need to spend quality time with God—away from distractions—where we have the chance to experience God's love for us. The only way I know how to accomplish this is through spending time with God, making ourselves available to the Holy Spirit, and practicing the lessons we learn.

Think It Through

Passages used to introduce "Acts of Discipleship": 2 Timothy 2:1–2; Mark 3:35

SIT
Choosing The Right Thing

"Show dogs don't sit!" the breeder stated emphatically when we brought Jazzy home. "They must stand at all times." Standing in a perfect stack is the sign of a champion (every breed has a standard by which all dogs of that breed are judged).

"I didn't know that you have to teach a dog to sit. I thought that they knew how to do that on their own." I should have left it alone, but I had to raise the ridiculous point if for no other reason than because it was a ridiculous point. Our breeder failed to see the humor in my statement. Instead, she went into a lengthy discourse about sitting and why it should be avoided. "Yes, it's natural, but it is not to be encouraged around you. If the dog relaxes in the ring, he might feel comfortable enough to sit, and we don't want that."

An interesting difference between show dogs and obedience dogs is that obedience dogs are strongly encouraged to sit. For an obedience dog, sitting is an essential element. Once a dog has completed a task, they are to return to their master's side, sit, and eagerly wait for the next command.

> We need to decide whether our relationship with God is going to be based on show or inspired by obedience. The decisions that we make will determine our actions and attitudes.

On the week when the puppy kindergarten instructor taught the sit command, we had to inform her that our dog could not learn to sit. I should point out that at the very time we said this to the instructor, Jazzy was sitting. The instructor took it in stride and tried to alter the program to fit the needs of our "show dog." The rest of the class spent their hour learning the sit command. At various times through the hour, however, I found myself wishing that I could sit.

Sitting is a universal concept. Every culture sits, and nearly all animals sit. My desert tortoise has the limitations of a heavy shell and short legs, but she understands what it means to sit. Whenever we are in the backyard, she comes to find us. She likes to sit close beside us because she knows we will give her roses and other flowers from areas higher than she can reach herself. In the summer, she follows us through the raised planter beds, knowing that along the way, we will pick a tomato, a zucchini, or some other delectable treat to place before her. By sitting at our feet, she knows that she will receive a great banquet.

We have the promise that God has set up a banqueting table and prepared a feast for us. This banquet is filled with blessings that we cannot reach on our own. We must come to Jesus, sit at his feet, and receive what he has for us. In the New Testament, we find the story of two sisters—Mary and Martha. Luke 10:38–42 tells us that Jesus was passing through the city where Mary and Martha lived. Though they were from the same family, their response to Jesus was very different. Jesus sat down and began to teach. Martha felt the need to work. There were refreshments to prepare, hosting to be done, needs to meet, and no one else to do the work. So Martha got to work. Mary, on the other hand, made the decision that she was going to sit at Jesus' feet and listen to what he had to say.

Martha felt justified by her activities. The work needed to be done. In fact, there was more work than Martha could accomplish by herself. So she approached Jesus while he was teaching and began to protest, "Tell Mary to help me! She has left all of the work of preparation and serving to me. It's not fair!"

Spiritual people don't sit. They work. We *know* this

is not true, but it *feels* like it to those who have fallen into the activity trap. It is so easy to talk about all of the things that you do, the positions that you fill, and the titles that you have as proof of your spiritual life. This scripture is a great reminder because we tend to feel like Jesus wants our service all the time. Yet Jesus does not see it that way. He wants us to be comfortable with him so that we willingly sit at his feet. This is what Mary did. She took a seat in the presence of Jesus and listened to him. "Martha, Martha, you are worried and bothered about so many things; but only a few things are necessary, really only one, for Mary has chosen the good part, which shall not be taken away" (Luke 10:41–42).

Are you choosing the good part? Or more importantly, where is your focus? The church is filled with tasks that need to be done in order for the organization to run smoothly. Jesus is not giving us permission to do nothing. James reminds us of this by saying, "But prove yourselves doers of the word, and not merely hearers who delude themselves" (James 1:22). James later adds to this idea with a discussion that faith must lead to actions.

The key is to find a balance between listening and doing. God wants us to sit at his feet. We cannot do what we haven't learned. If we are so busy showing ourselves to be spiritual, then we are on a crash course to burnout. But if we take the time to sit at Jesus' feet and listen to his teaching, we are filling the well from which our service springs.

In Luke chapter 9, Jesus went up to the mountain

to pray. Peter, James, and John went along with him. As Jesus prayed, he went through a change. He began to glow with the radiance of God. As this happened, Moses and Elijah appeared and carried on a conversation with Jesus. What a tremendous experience! Could you imagine being in this situation? What would you do if you were Peter, James, or John?

I believe Peter did what most of us would do. He started to talk. His talking led to plans that he could implement to commemorate the experience. Apparently, Peter was only interested in what he could see. It was a pretty incredible sight, but Peter was completely missing all that could be heard. So God had to take away the visual by laying a large cloud over the group so that Peter could no longer see what was going on. Then the voice of God lanced through the clouds saying, "This is My Son, My Chosen One, listen to Him" (Luke 9:35).

We are not much different from Peter. Most people are visually oriented. We look at people. We look for people that we know. We scan the church auditorium to make sure that everything is in place and looks good. But how much of the pastor's sermon do we remember?

The Bible tells us that God has called people to ministry. He has given them specific gifts to accomplish that ministry. The preaching of the Word is one way that the Lord will speak to us. Our job as believers is to approach the sermon with the expectation that God has something special to share with us. It may only be one small point in the sermon, but if you hear it and receive it, then you have something great to work on through the week.

Do you have a time in your day when you can sit down with God and listen? We fill our calendars with appointments, and we fill in the free time with things that must be done around the house. The television provides constant noise and visual stimulus, numbing our minds from the worries of the day. In the midst of all of this, God wants to communicate with us. When we do take the opportunity to pray, we do all of the talking, plowing through our prayer list so that we can move on to the next item on our calendar. Yet if we are doing all of the talking, what chance does God have to commune with us? Reading Scripture and praying is essential in your quiet time. Being able to sit quietly and listen is just as important.

Think It Through

Passages used to illustrate "Sit": Luke 10:38–42; James 1:22; Luke 9:28–35.

On Your Own

Luke chapter 8 records a story of a man who had many demons. Jesus cast the demons from the man into a herd of pigs. As a result, the pigs turned and ran off a cliff and drowned in the Sea of Galilee. The local residents were frustrated that their swine business had been wiped out and came to ask Jesus to leave. What they found is recorded in Luke 8:35: "And the people went out to see what had happened and they came to Jesus, and found the man from whom the demons had gone out, sitting down at the feet of Jesus." This formerly possessed man was well known by the crowd. He was a wild man who lived among the graves. But there he was sitting calmly before the one who healed him. From that point on, the man walked among his people, telling anyone who would listen about the wonderful things that Jesus had done for him.

How has the Lord demonstrated his love for you? How has he cleansed you from the struggles you once faced?

_____

_____

_____

Read Psalm 1:1–3. Consider your daily schedule and evaluate the things that you hold as important. Are you securely seated before the Lord like a tree firmly planted, or are you reacting more to those who would scoff at your faith?

Psalm 26:1–7 records a powerful prayer seeking vindication and support. The prayer leads to a declaration to fully trust the Lord. Read through this passage several times and turn it into your own prayer of dedication.

LEAVE IT
Yielding Authority

Before reading any more of this book, take a few minutes to create a list. Get a pencil and paper and complete this simple task. First, make a list of the things that are most important to you. List all of the things that come to your mind. You will be surprised how many important things are taking up residence in your mind.

Next, give each of the items on the list a number value, one being the most important thing in your life. This may be a difficult task, but do the best you can. It might help to think of it as a list of things that must be done in a day. Which item would you make sure was accomplished first?

Now make a second list. This list should be the things that keep you from reaching your top priorities. List the temptations, the personal struggles, or the circumstances that keep your mind off of those most important things. Your list will probably include items that are not bad but simply distracting.

(If you are reading this paragraph, and you have completed your two lists, then please read on. If you have not, then stop now and do it. The point of this book is to grow in the Lord, not simply to make it to the last page. There is a point to this experience, and if you read on, you will miss it.)

Now that you have created your two lists, it is time to compare them. Are there specific challenges that draw your focus from something that is important to you? Draw a line between those two things or rewrite the list so that the important item and the distraction are next to each other. Make the comparison whichever way it works best for you. Just make sure that you know what challenges are keeping you from being successful at the things that are most important.

Jesus seemed to address the conflict that we feel between our two lists. Recorded in Matthew 10, Jesus said,

> "Do not think that I came to bring peace on the earth; I did not come to bring peace, but a sword. For I came to set a man against his father, and a daughter against her mother, and a daughter-in-law

against her mother-in-law; and a man's enemies will be the members of his household. He who loves father or mother more than Me is not worthy of Me; and he who loves son or daughter more than Me is not worthy of Me. And he who does not take his cross and follow after Me is not worthy of me. He who has found his life shall lose it, and he who has lost his life for My sake shall find it."

Matthew 1:34–39

If Jesus were to use the terminology used in puppy kindergarten, he would say, "Leave it!"

On the week we practiced the "leave it" command, we were told to bring lots of small treats. The smell of a meaty treat provides motivation for dogs. Smell is the strongest sense a dog has. Before their eyes or ears ever opened, their sense of smell was acute. Because of this, smell remains a vital part of a dog's awareness throughout their life.

Each partnership of dog and master was instructed to walk through the aisles of the pet store under the watchful eye of our teacher. "As you walk, drop a treat in front of your dog and tell them to leave it. If they move toward the treat, add tension to the leash and repeat the command." For the next half hour, teams of dogs and owners moved about the store, dropping treats and saying "leave it" in our most authoritative voices. Eventually, there were so many treats on the floor that we did not need to drop anything new. The store was like a minefield of enticing smells. Obeying meant leaving the food on the floor and trusting their master. In scriptural terms, going for the food is walking by sight. Trusting the master is walking by faith.

The "leave it" command is very important in the relationship between owner and dog. <u>It is the owner that has the reasoning skills to know when a dog is going after something that would be detrimental to their health.</u> As the master, it is our job to protect our pets from harm. Telling a dog to "leave it" sets us up as the owner of the goody and allows us to control when or if the dog gets to enjoy the treat. But the most important reason for the "leave it" command is that it forces the dog to make a decision: do I want the treat, or do I want to obey my master? Which do I want more? As the dog learns to follow the command, the owner can add another command: take it!

Some of the issues that we face in life are not wrong, sinful, or even harmful. God does not take things away from us simply to be harsh. He does not say no to our requests just to prove that he is bigger than we are. Certainly, there are times when God knows more than we do. He sees the future, and he knows what will bring us harm. Our God loves us enough to say *no* to our requests. He says "leave it" when we get too close to things that would draw us away from our relationship with him.

> There are times when God says, "Leave it," because we need to make a decision. Do we want our relationship with Jesus more than we want the desire that has taken its place in our heart?

Jesus knows the key to eternal life. "He who loves his life loses it, and he who hates his life in this world shall keep it to life eternal" (John 12:25). The big question is what takes first place in your heart? Where are your priorities? Jesus speaks to the importance of answering this question in Matthew 6:24: "No one can serve two masters; for either he will hate the one and love the other, or he will hold to one and despise the other. You cannot serve God and mammon." He drives the same point home in Matthew 16:26, "For whoever wishes to save his life shall lose it; but whoever loses his life for My sake shall find it."

When we face temptation, Jesus says, "Leave it." When our priorities are out of focus, Jesus says, "Leave it." Yet there are times when Jesus says "leave it" under very ordinary circumstances. It may be an offer of a good job, or a one-time-only great deal. The offers sound good, but something tells you not to take it. That feeling is usually a direct result of God saying, "Leave it." It is at those times that we must believe God has something else for us to do. Such was the case with the calling of the disciples.

> "And walking by the Sea of Galilee, He saw two brothers, Simon who was called Peter, and Andrew his brother, casting a net into the sea; for they were fishermen. And He said to them, 'Follow Me, and I will make you fishers of men.' And they immediately left their nets, and followed Him. And going on from there He saw two other brothers, James the son of Zebedee, and John his brother, in the boat

with Zebedee their father, mending their nets; and He called them. And they immediately left the boat and their father and followed Him"

Matthew 4:18–22

There is nothing wrong with being a fisherman, mending nets, and being very good at your job. We honor the Lord when we give our best to everything we do. Paul urged Titus by saying, "Remind them to be subject to rulers, to authorities, to be obedient, to be ready for every good deed, to malign no one, to be uncontentious, gentle, showing every consideration for all good men" (Titus 3:1–2). Yet when God says, "leave it," are you are prepared to walk away?

I was invited to fly from Idaho to Texas, where a church was considering me to become their pastor. Kim and I had never been to Texas before, and the prospect of working with this church was very appealing. We had a great time of fellowship with the people and felt that the match could be a very good one. After Sunday services, Kim and I boarded a plane and headed back to Idaho. The church made the commitment to have the congregation vote about inviting me to pastor the church and get back to us soon. When we arrived at our house late Sunday evening, the phone was already ringing. I rushed in, dropped the bags, and answered the phone. It was a leader from the church in Texas. He thanked us for coming, told us how much the church enjoyed our visit, and told us that we were everything that they wanted in a minister. Then he informed us that the church had voted not to call us. They were bewildered with the vote. We were stunned with the results, but the Lord had clearly said, "Leave it."

Not long after our disappointing trip to Texas, Kim and I were invited to serve a struggling church in Southern California. It was very different than the healthy looking church in Texas, but we believed that God had opened the door, and we gladly accepted the call. The circumstances that seemed so odd at the time became clear over the next few years. The struggling California church went on to be a healthy, thriving congregation. The healthy Texas church split within a couple of years, struggled for a while, and eventually closed its doors.

<u>What do you do when God's will and your plans do not match?</u> Do you trust his word, or try to sneak the goody anyway in hopes that he will bless your disobedience? It doesn't matter that the idea looks good on paper or that you have made a significant investment in the project. When God says, "leave it," can you walk away trusting that God's will is better than the best plan you can dream up? If you do not trust His will, you will struggle to find His blessings in your life.

Think It Through

Passages used to illustrate "Leave It": Matthew 10:34; John 12:25; Matthew 6:24; Matthew 16:26; Matthew 4:18–22; Titus 3:1–2.

On Your Own

Meditate on the following Psalm, "For every beast of the forest is Mine, the cattle on a thousand hills.

* Jer 29 v. 13 "--- with all your heart"

I know every bird of the mountains, and everything that moves in the fields is Mine. If I were hungry, I would not tell you; For the world is Mine, and all it contains" (Psalm 50:10–11). What does this passage say about God's authority?

_____

_____

_____

Answer the same question as you read Luke 14:26–27—"If anyone comes to Me, and does not hate his own father and mother and wife and children and brothers and sisters, yes and even his own life, he cannot be My disciple. Whoever does not carry his own cross and come after Me cannot be My disciple."

_____

_____

_____

Can you think of a time when God said "leave it," and you obeyed His will? What happened?

_____

_____

_____

Can you think of a time when God said, "leave it," but you followed your own plan anyway? How did that work out?

How can you apply the words of Psalm 84:10 to your own life? "For a day in Thy courts is better than a thousand outside. I would rather stand at the threshold of the house of my God, than dwell in the tents of wickedness.

TAKE IT
Trust the One Who Knows

Animal trainers are quick to tell us that dogs live in the moment. They do not remember individual experiences, and they do not hold a grudge against their owners. They do, however, develop conditioned responses to situations. They learn to be aggressive or fearful to counteract external stimulus. Once a dog discovers that a certain response works in a situation, they will return to that response over and over. The problem is that owners have vivid memories of past experiences. We remember a traumatic situation long after the event has taken place. Animal owners say that they feel sorry for their pet or are protective of their pet because they remember a hurt from the past. Whatever it is that they remember, they don't want it to happen again. Those feelings translate into projected energy. Our dogs read and react to it. We have created that response because we are not able to move beyond the pain of the past. Yet if we live in the moment and change our approach to the negative circumstance, our dog will follow with positive behavior. <u>Base your leadership on a positive present</u>, <u>not on the painful past</u>. You will find yourself working with a well-balanced dog that you will enjoy rewarding with our next command, "Take it."

Shortly after our son was married, he and his wife brought home a cute little chocolate Labrador they called Moose. They loved him and taught him to perform lots of tricks. They taught him to fetch and took him to a local pond to express his retriever instincts. Although they did not use the words *take it,* they certainly taught him the meaning of the command. Whenever they would present Moose with a bowl of food, Moose would lower his head patiently in front of his bowl. They would ask God to bless the food, ending with the words *In Jesus' name, amen.*

Moose learned that those words meant that the prayer was over and he was now free to take it. Moose never looked down at the food and wondered if he was worthy enough to receive it. He may have dug a hole in the middle of the lawn, left tooth marks in a patio chair, or knocked the lamp off of the end table; yet none of those experiences declared him an unworthy dog. He was made worthy by the acceptance of his master and the offer of the food. The good news of the gospel is that God has many wonderful blessings in store for those who commit to Jesus and receive the gifts that he has to offer. By faith, God wants us to take it!

On the day we added the "take it" command in puppy kindergarten, our instructor stood back, carefully watching both animal and owner. From time to time, she would question specific actions of an owner. "Well, I know my dog, and he always acts this way," said the owner of an active mixed-breed dog. Our instructor tactfully disagreed with the owner's assessment, took the leash, and repeated the activity that triggered the anxiety between owner and dog. Sure enough, the dog followed the command and stood calmly by the instructor. When she said, "leave it," the dog obeyed. The same happened with come, sit, down, and anything else she asked from the dog. It was as if she had gone around the corner and switched dogs. All of the owners in puppy kindergarten had the same response, "How did she do that?"

The instructor did not have negative memories of the past. She had no expectations of failure based on past events. She just wanted the dog to follow her command. Because she was projecting a positive, yet commanding energy, the dog had a completely different response.

Many years ago, I was impressed by the relationship between my father-in-law and one of his many dogs. Jim managed vineyards in the Napa Valley and found that having a dog came in handy as he walked the vast fields of grapes.

One day, Jim went to the business office that was in

the vineyard owner's home. The owner had two young fox terriers that lived on the property. The dogs, named Joker and Domino, were brothers from the same litter, and they loved to play rough. When Jim arrived, he saw that Joker was missing. He searched until he found the dog, which had fallen off of a deck and was impaled on a fence by one leg. Jim rescued the dog and rushed him to the animal hospital. The dog was resilient and regained his health, but the leg could not be saved. Through this experience, a bond was formed, and the grateful three-legged dog became Jim's constant companion. What impressed me about their relationship was that Jim never treated Joker differently because he had lost a leg. Jim focused on the parts that were still there and found tremendous value in their companionship.

The three-legged dog was well known around his small town. If Jim went to town and did not take him, the dog would set off on his own to find his master. He knew all of Jim's hangouts and would visit them, one by one, until dog and master were reunited. The three-legged dog was accepted everywhere that Jim went. Often, the owners of the businesses kept treats for Jim's dog. If Joker couldn't find Jim, he would go to city hall, where he knew he could count on a ride home in one of the town's police cars.

One day, Jim traveled to his boss's ranch, about an hour from his house. Joker noticed him leaving and jumped in to ride along. When they reached their destination, Jim went into a house. Joker remained outside to explore the area. When Jim left, the dog was nowhere in sight, so the owner of the house agreed to bring the dog home. As Jim arrived home, however, he was amazed to find his three-legged companion sleeping on the porch. How he got there remains a mystery. Had he been just any dog, he may have been left on the side of the road. But this was Jim's dog, and everybody knew it. Undoubtedly, someone saw him as they drove by and brought the three-legged dog home to his master.

As I considered this relationship, several ideas impressed me. First, Jim's dog was shaped by his past, but he was not controlled by it. In fact, it made him special. Second, the dog did not focus on what wasn't there (his fourth leg). His focus was on the man who saw his future and helped him live it. And finally, no matter how far he wandered, the three-legged dog knew where he belonged and always returned to the master that saw value in saving him.

You may be shaped by the struggles of your past, but by the grace of God you do not need to be controlled by those struggles. Isaiah 43:25 says, "I, even I, am the one who wipes out your transgressions for My own sake; and I will not remember your sins." This promise was restated in Hebrews 8:12, "For I will be merciful to their iniquities, and I will remember their sins no more." We know these words are true, but all too often we are unable to enjoy the peace and security that God has promised us. We struggle with guilt. We accept that negative things will happen to us now because they happened to us in the past. We hold ourselves captive by negative experiences. We do not forgive ourselves! We struggle with low spiritual self-esteem, unable to grasp the truth that God, through

Jesus, has forgiven us and forgotten our past. When we stop listening to the past and accept the truth of God's forgiveness, then we can finally begin to experience a very powerful lesson from puppy kindergarten: take it.

The single adult ministry program at our church has claimed the promises of Jeremiah.

> "'For I know the plans that I have for you,' declares the Lord, 'plans for welfare and not for calamity to give you a future and a hope. Then you will call upon Me and come and pray to Me, and I will listen to you."
>
> Jeremiah 29:11–12

Many of the members of our group have had difficulties in the past. They have experienced their share of heartache, loss, trials, and discouragement. No doubt you have experienced some of those things as well. Yet they are trusting Jesus to keep His promises. They have been shaped by their experiences, but they are not controlled by them. Instead, they follow the one who saw their need for salvation and desire to have a loving relationship with them. They have chosen to take the focus off of what is no longer there and focus their attention on the one who saw value in them. They have made the commitment to trust God's call to "take it." Their desire is to follow the testimony of the Apostle Paul, who said, "Brethren, I do not regard myself as having laid hold of it yet; but one thing I do; forgetting what lies behind and reaching forward to what lies ahead, I press on toward the goal for the prize of the upward call of God in Christ Jesus" (Philippians 3:13–14).

The question is, what does he want you to take?

"But as many as received Him, to them He gave the right to become children of God, even to those who believe in His name, were born not of blood, nor of the will of the flesh, nor of the will of man but of God" (John 1:12–13). Salvation is yours. Take it.

"These things I have spoken to you, while abiding with you. But the Helper, the Holy Spirit, whom the Father will send in My name, He will teach you all things, and bring to your remembrance all that I said to you" (John 14:25–26). The Holy Spirit is yours. Take it.

"In Him we have redemption through His blood, the forgiveness of our trespasses, according to the riches of His Grace which He lavished upon us" (Ephesians 1:7–8). Forgiveness is yours. Take it.

> "Look at the birds of the air, that they do not sow, neither do they reap, nor gather into barns, and yet your heavenly Father feeds them. Are you not worth much more than they? And which of you by being anxious can add a single cubit to his life's span? And why are you anxious about clothing? Observe how the lilies of the field grow; they do not toil nor do they spin, yet I say to you that even Solomon in all his glory did not clothe himself like one of these. But if God so arrays the grass of the field, which is alive today and tomorrow is thrown into the furnace, will He not much more do so for you, O men of little faith?"
>
> Matthew 6:25–30

God's provisions are yours. Take it.

Psalm 84:11–12, "For the Lord God is a sun and shield; the Lord gives grace and glory; No good thing does He withhold from those who walk uprightly. O Lord of hosts, how blessed is the man who trusts in Thee!" Every promise of the Scripture is yours. Take it.

Because our dogs live in the present, when we change our approach, they change their behavior. Their response comes from what's happening now, not from the pain and guilt of past mistakes. By grace, we are not bound by the pain and guilt of the past either. Accept God's forgiveness. Forgive yourself. Change your approach, and your life will begin the dramatic transformation that comes to those who believe Jesus.

Think It Through

Passages used in "Take It": Isaiah 43:25; Hebrews 8:12; Jeremiah 29:11–12; Philippians 3:13–14; John 1:12–13; John 14:25–26; Ephesians 1:7–8; Matthew 6:25–30; Psalm 84:11–12.

On Your Own

Ephesians 6:10–20 creates a picture of several things God wants us to take. Read through this text and write a list of the items. Find a study guide on this chapter or try an Internet search on how they apply to your spiritual life. What do you need to take? Why it is important that you "take it"?

_____

_____

_____

Acts of Faithfulness

Maintaining command of your dog requires that they master one overarching command. With all that is available to draw their attention away from us, we need to insure that they are focused on us. Trees to check, kids to chase, other dogs to get to know, things to sniff, and movement everywhere threaten to tempt them to inappropriate behavior. This is why a considerable amount of time is spent with the *look* command. The teacher had us bring our treats and have our puppy sit in front of us. While holding the treat near our face, we practiced the *look* command. The puppy would see the treat and focus on our face. As we practiced, the puppy would see us instead of the treat. Eventually, the treat didn't need to be there. When we said, "look," our dogs would face us and watch for the next command. The only way for a dog to act faithfully toward his or her master is to develop the ability to tune out all other distractions and maintain their focus.

We cannot be faithful to the Lord with our attention on every distraction that comes our way. We must look to the Lord, confident that he has a plan for us. This is why Peter wrote, "Therefore, gird your minds for action, keep sober in spirit, fix your hope completely on the grace to be brought to you at the revelation of Jesus Christ" (1 Peter 1:13). Paul urged Titus to constantly be "looking for the blessed hope and the appearing of the glory of our great God and Savior, Christ Jesus" (Titus 2:13). The writer of Hebrews created a word picture to help us with this concept.

> "Therefore, since we have so great a cloud of witnesses surrounding us, let us lay aside every circumstance, and the sin which so easily entangles us, and let us run with endurance the race that is set before us, fixing our eyes on Jesus, the author and perfector of faith, who for the joy set before Him endured the cross, despising the shame, and has sat down at the right hand of the throne of God."
>
> Hebrews 12:1

As we learn to look, we gain confidence to follow the last three commands of puppy kindergarten—come, wait, and stay. These three commands are keys to faithfulness.

Think It Through

Passages used to illustrate "Acts of Faithfulness": 1 Peter 1:13; Titus 2:13; Hebrews 12:1.

COME
Your Source of Strength

Shortly after Kim and I were married, I brought home a cute little puppy (the result of several trips to the humane society shelter). Toots (a nickname I had attributed to Kim while we were dating) became an instant part of our family. She had long, glistening white hair and large brown spots. I used to take her with me to the church (my first youth ministry), where she would sit at my feet under the desk. She enjoyed hanging her head out of the car window, feeling the breeze rush past her face. At times, she would push the limits and stretch her body too far out of the window. I would warn her, and she would respond by pulling herself back into the car. One day, on the way home from the church, we pulled up to a traffic light. There must have been a wonderful scent in the air because she nearly fell out of the passenger window. Without thinking, I turned and spoke with a loud voice to get her attention. I did not notice that an elderly woman had pulled into the lane next to me. Her window was also open. When I looked in her direction, and yelled, "Hey, Toots," she thought I was talking to her. The light could not have changed fast enough.

We have enjoyed pure and mixed breed dogs in our home. Some came to us as puppies, and others were rescues.

One day, when our children were young, we visited the local animal shelter. I don't even know how we ended up there. All I know is that a cute little dog caught our eye. We were told that she was a stray, a rescue, or, as the shelter employee called her, a runner. We named her Buffy. We chose her, but she never chose us. The slightest crack in a fence, a tiny hole under the gate, a door left ajar, and she was gone on a dead run. Buffy was apparently a regular at the shelter. It didn't matter how much money we spent on her, she was not interested in being a part of our family. Her life was cut short while crossing a busy street on one of her adventures.

There are times when we all feel like Buffy. God has offered us his love and life in his eternal home, yet we run, trying to satisfy our desire to control our own lives. Hymn writer Robert Robinson must have felt the same way when he penned the chorus of "Come Thou Fount of Every Blessing."

> "Prone to wander, Lord, I feel it,
> Prone to leave the God I love;
> Here's my heart, O take and seal it,
> Seal it for Thy courts above."

It seems like our wandering takes two forms. We wander for reasons, and we wander for seasons.

There are no good reasons for wandering away from the Lord, but we try to justify them nevertheless. Yet from time to time, our focus is drawn away from the Lord. The Bible identifies these distractions as stumbling blocks. The adversary knows our weaknesses and works to exploit them at every turn. Perhaps this is why the Apostle Paul confessed that he needed to die daily to himself, that he may be alive to Christ. It is so easy to take our eyes off of the prize, but with each wandering, Christ promises a "way of escape" (1 Corinthians 10:13). To those who are trying to justify their wandering Jesus says, "Come."

There are other times when we wander for a season. The length of the season changes, but the root remains the same. Galatians 6:1 says, "Brethren, even if a man is caught in any trespass, you who are spiritual, restore such a one in a spirit of gentleness; each one looking to yourself, lest you too be tempted." Think of being caught as being stuck, snagged, unable to free oneself, or needing the help of others. Our season may be nothing more than a prolonged dry spell where we feel parched instead of quenched. Our relationship with Jesus feels more like a religious ritual void of renewal. Seasons of wandering also have their way of escape. If we allow God to reach us, He will bring spiritual people into our path to help bring restoration to our soul. These people will help us, "Repent, therefore, and return, that your sins may be wiped away, in order that times of refreshing may come from the presence of the Lord" (Acts 3:19). Whether our wandering is for a reason or a season, God is calling out to us, "Come."

When Kim took Satchmo (our male Australian terrier) to obedience class, she was told to invest in a leash with a thirty-foot lead. Within the range of his sixty-foot circle, Satchmo had free will. He could choose to come or to wander. At the center of the circle, holding the other end of the lead, was his master. She began by calling his name, showing him a treat, and saying, "Come." As he recognized his name, Satchmo learned that coming when invited had very tasty rewards. The next step was to call him without showing the treat, only revealing it when he came. Ultimately, he came when called for nothing more than the praise and affection of his master. The desired response to "come" is that our dog comes joyfully because they have the confidence that something wonderful will follow.

Jesus said much the same thing to those who were at the end of their ropes.

> "Come to Me, all who are weary and heavy-laden, and I will give you rest. Take My yoke upon you, and learn from Me, for I am gentle and humble in

heart; and you shall find rest for your souls. For My yoke is easy, and My load is light."

Matthew 11:28–30

These words are condensed from a passage that His listeners would have understood well. In Isaiah 55, God lays out His plan for us.

"Ho! Everyone who thirsts, come to the waters; and you who have no money come, buy and eat. Come, buy wine and milk without money and without cost. Why do you spend money for what is not bread, and your wages for what does not satisfy? Listen carefully to Me, and eat what is good, and delight yourself in abundance. Incline your ear and come to me. Listen, that you may live; and I will make an everlasting covenant with you according to the faithful mercies shown to David."

Isaiah 55:1–3

God's plan has never changed. Whether Jesus was quoting Scripture or speaking in public, the message never changed.

"Now on the last day of the great feast, Jesus stood and cried out, saying, 'If any man is thirsty, let him come to Me and drink. He who believes in Me, as the Scripture said, from the innermost being shall flow rivers of living water.'"

John 7:37–38

If you are at the end of your rope, weary from your wandering, know that Jesus is still close by, waiting for you to turn back to him. He is opening His hand, freely offering His gift of life, and calling you to "Come."

Think It Through

Passages used to illustrate "Come": 1 Corinthians 10:13; Galatians 6:1; Acts 3:19; Matthew 11:28–30; Isaiah 55:1–3; John 7:37–38

On Your Own

Psalm 66 turns the concept of *come* into a celebration. There are two specific calls to come. By coming, we are able to see and hear what God has for us. List the things that God wants us to see and the things he wants us to hear.

_____

_____

_____

Matthew 25:31–46 takes a prophetic look at the second coming of Christ. This passage looks toward a call to come that we do not want to miss. When you read through this passage, pay close attention to the behaviors of those who receive the invitation. Think about the question, "What is God calling you to do?" When the call to come is made, will you be ready?

_____

_____

_____

WAIT
Trusting God's Timing

My friend Lisa and her chocolate Lab were spending time relaxing together. Ginger was settled and completely focused on her master. As Ginger remained in the down position, Lisa took two treats and placed one atop each of Ginger's front paws. "Wait," she urged. Ginger glanced at the treats, then back at Lisa, repeating each step several times. She needed to trust her master's timing, but the tempting treats resting gently on each forefoot were hard to ignore. The difficulty with the experience was that Ginger knew the treats were hers, but the timing was up to Lisa. Ginger was committed to wait. If she moved toward the treats, Lisa would take them away. So she waited and waited. Saliva formed around the sides of her mouth as she considered the promised goodies. Finally, when the time was right, Lisa gave her permission to take it. How sweet those treats must have been for Ginger, who trusted her master and received her blessing. The wait command is very important because it allows the master to control three major areas.

The wait command allows the dog to maintain their level of trust for the owner. Our dogs have an inherent pack mentality. A chain of command is essential for them to feel comfortable in any environment. They need to know who is in control. Many owners think that their dogs want to be in control. This is not necessarily the case. Dogs have no trouble giving up control to their owners when they are presented with confident leadership. Your dog will yield to your authority when they trust your energy. Their trust will increase incrementally as you are consistent with your leadership.

The wait command also allows the owner to control the energy of their dog. This is important when it is time to feed the dog or when we take out the leash. Presenting the stimulus can raise a dog's energy level dramatically. If the energy level is not controlled, the dog will maintain a high energy level and become more and more distressed. Wait helps a dog to maintain a calm state so that the activity becomes a pleasant experience, and both dog and owner will be able to move on to the next activity in harmony.

Finally, the wait command allows the owner to control the behavior of his or her dog. When you open the front door of your house, you do not want your pet to dart outside unattended. You may be taking them out, but you need to have control over them before they go outside. It is difficult to get control back once all of the sights and smells of the outside world hit their nose. Wait will allow you to lead your dog outside instead of them leading you.

> How do you react when you know that a blessing is yours, yet God is clearly saying, "Wait"? Can you trust the Lord even though the prayer is not answered yet? Maybe the job has not been offered, your soul mate hasn't arrived yet, or your children have not yet come to the Lord. God's promises are yours, but it is clear that you must wait.

Do you begin to question your trust in God's plan? Do you find subtle ways of taking back control of your life so that you can make things happen on your time? Does the fact that you must wait tempt you to engage in behavior that does not bring glory to the Lord? Answering these three questions honestly can be very convicting.

God wants us to be faithful to him. This means we must look to him for direction, and wait for his perfect timing. Isaiah wrote, "Yet those who wait for the Lord will gain new strength; they will mount up with wings like eagles, they will run and not get tired, they will walk and not become weary" (Isaiah 40:31). When God opens a door, it is not our job to rush through and do whatever we want. Our job is to trust him (Hebrews 2:13), let His love "control us" (2 Corinthians 5:14), and behave "in a manner worthy of our calling" (Ephesians 4:1). As this happens, the blessing of the open door will bring joy, peace, and fulfillment.

Perhaps you are remembering the many times you have tried to "wait" upon the Lord and were frustrated. Nothing seemed to happen, or you went ahead without him and made a mess of things on your own. At these times, we don't need to be reminded that our timing rarely matches God's. We are so finite, and he is infinite. He sees everything, while we only see what is right before us. He moves in ways that make no sense to us, and it can be difficult to keep our eyes upon him when the things we desire are right near our grasp.

Maybe God is just slow. Peter addressed this idea by saying, "The Lord is not slow about His promise, as some count slowness, but is patient toward you…" (2 Peter 3:12). The old praise chorus reminds us, "He makes all things beautiful in His time." This is followed by a prayer offered in the chorus, "Lord please show me every day, as you're teaching me your way, that you do just what you say, in your time" (*In His Time,* Diane Ball).

It's possible that God is saying "Wait" because you are not ready to receive the gift that he has prepared for you? He knows the areas where growth must still take place. He wants to give you the blessing, but you must be ready to receive it. So you "Wait." Ask yourself this question: "Can I be spiritually strong without the blessing so that I will remain spiritually faithful with it?" Your relationship with the Lord cannot be dependant upon whether or not you receive the blessings you desire in your heart.

Has your desire for the blessing become more important than your desire to draw close to God? Has the blessing become your stumbling block? What needs to change before the blessing can be granted to you? Where do you need to grow so that the Lord can freely say "Take It"?

> "The Lord sustains all who fall, and raises up all who are bowed down. The eyes of all look to Thee, and Thou dost give them their food in due time. Thou dost open Thy hand, and dost satisfy the desire of every living thing."
>
> Psalm 145:14–16

These words were written to give you hope in the times when you stop looking at Christ and rush through the door on your own. He is there to pick you up again and set your feet back on the path of righteousness. Remember the words of Proverbs 24:16, "For a righteous man falls seven times, and rises again, but the wicked stumble in time of calamity." Notice that the righteous and the unrighteous both stumble. The difference between the two is their response. It is the person of faith that is able to rise up again.

Abram was promised a son, but to receive the fulfillment of that promise, he had to wait. Moses led the children of Israel out of Egypt, but because they strayed, they ended up having to wait forty years to receive their promise. David was anointed king at a very young age but had to wait a long time before God led him through that door. Paul felt the call to go to Macedonia, but God made him wait. The Scripture is filled with stories of those who had to wait for an open door. If it happened for them, why are we so impatient when it happens to us?

From time to time, my family likes to play miniature golf. We have a great time, and the game can become fairly competitive. On nearly every miniature golf course that I have seen is some variation of the trap door. The giant castle looms before you with a small opening at the bottom. Covering the ramp to the castle is a door that mechanically rises and falls. The timing of the door is designed to trick you. Our tendency is to watch the door and swing when it begins to open. If we do this, then we can be certain that the door will be closed by the time the ball arrives at the ramp. Ricochet off the door a time or two, and you learn that you need to trust the consistency of the door and swing at the ball while the door is shut. By the time your golf ball arrives, the door is open.

The mechanical door is a fun part of miniature golf, but it is not a part of God's plan. He does not tempt us, try to fake us out, and then slam the door in our face as we make our approach. If there is anything that rises and falls, it is our faith. God, on the other hand, has thrown open the door. If He is saying, "wait," it is because we are not ready. It is then that we should check our level of trust, consider if we are trying to control things on our own and are behaving in a way that brings Him glory. Gain control of these three areas, and you will find many new doors open to you.

Think It Through

Passages used to illustrate "Wait": Isaiah 40:31; Hebrews 2:13; 2 Corinthians 5:14; Ephesians 4:1; 2 Peter 3:12; Psalm 145:14–16; Proverbs 24:16.

On Your Own

Read the words of Exodus 32. God led the people of Israel to this place. He had opened the door to a new level of relationship with them. What happened to create such disarray? The answer is found in verse 25. What was lost, and what did Moses do about it in verse 26?

_____

_____

_____

STAY
Spiritually Strong in Tough Times

Wait and stay. Aren't these two commands different ways of saying the same thing? No. With the wait command, a dog can move, sit, stand, wag their tail, or any other thing they want to do. They are just not allowed to carry out that one specific behavior, occupy the space, or walk out the door. Stay, on the other hand, means "Do not move." Stay means there is danger, a problem, or a situation that requires the dog to trust you and follow your command completely.

Stay begins in puppy kindergarten. Instructors usually have us encourage the puppy to sit in front of us. We slowly move back, repeating the stay command over and over. When we get to the end of the lead, we repeat the command again. This is followed by a release word. I actually use the word *release* with my own dogs. Dogs know that obeying the stay command is followed by a rewarding release. As the dog ages, the duration of their ability to stay increases. As you and your pet continue through the levels of obedience class, the challenge increases as well. They may issue a sit or down command, followed by stay. The owner will then disappear around a corner or hide behind some object and wait. Success means that a dog told to stay will not move, even when their owner is out of sight.

Dog experts remind us that the stay command must always be given with intentionality, a time frame, and a specific release command. Many owners confuse wait with stay. They go to the door, tell their dog to stay, and then leave for several hours. Do they intend for the dog to remain in the same position while they do all of their shopping? No, the just didn't want them to run out the door. What they really meant was, "Wait." The dog can move around, take a nap, or pace the floor, but they cannot walk out the door. The problem with using *stay* when we really mean *wait* comes when the dog discovers that they can get up and move around without recourse. They quickly learn that obedience to stay ends when the door closes. Eventually, the dog will disregard stay as just another word that comes out of your mouth. This could be disastrous during a difficult situation. The stay command insures the safety of the dog. Obedience to stay means that our dog trusts us and remains submissive to our control.

God wants us trust him, and submit to his control. When we are told to "stay," we need to trust that God has a reason. He wants to keep us safe and desires for us to grow in faithfulness.

Often, we are expected to stay during difficult situations (which are probably the hardest times to stand strong). Psalm 23 paints a beautiful picture of life, reminding us that we are not ushered around the valley of the shadow of death but through it. This is why we must listen to Him, trust His Word, and grow through the experience.

The stay command is addressed through several New Testament words. Jesus used the word *abide,* which means "to dwell in, remain in, or stay." New Testament writers urged us to stand, which also means "to stay in one place, to dig in ones heels and not move from a certain position." So in this context, if a passage says abide or stand, it is God's way of saying, "Stay." In each passage, I will insert the word *stay,* not to change the scripture, but to help us remember that in this context, the words are being used interchangeably.

The biblical command to stay is given as a condition of our relationship with God. "Jesus therefore was saying to those Jews who had believed, 'If you abide (stay) in My word, then you are truly disciples of Mine; and you shall know the truth, and the truth shall make you free'" (John 8:31–32). Conversely, if we do not abide in Jesus, then we will not know the truth, and we will not know the freedom, which comes through that truth.

Understanding the freeing power of the truth comes with our next stay command. "If you abide (stay) in Me, and My words abide (stay) in you, ask whatever you wish, and it shall be done for you" (John 15:7). How do we stay close to Jesus? By staying in His word.

Early in ministry, I was preaching at a growing church in California. Before one Sunday morning service, one of the church leaders was giving a pep talk to those who were scheduled to serve that week. His discussion centered on his favorite verse and couldn't remember where it was. He was, however, able to quote the all-too-well-known verse, "God helps those who help themselves." When he released the group of workers, I took him aside and gently informed him that his favorite quotation was not in the Scripture at all. "Well, it should be," was his response.

How can we have a relationship with Christ and have no idea what is in his Word? How can we lead churches and not know what he said? We need to get into the Word and stay there. We must read through it, pray through it, practice it, and continue to stay, remain, and abide. Our freedom in Christ is dependant upon our abiding in his word.

Jesus continues with his stay commands: "Just as the Father has loved Me, I have also loved you; abide (stay) in My love. If you keep My commandments, you will abide in My love; just as I have kept My Father's commandments, and abide in His love" (John 15:9–10). The progression we are creating here should be evident. We are to stay with Jesus. We learn how to do that when we stay in his Word. As we do this, we come to understand the freedom that comes from a relationship with Jesus. As a result, we are able to stay in his love.

Wow, isn't this the place where we want to be? Paul understood this when he wrote to the believers in Philippi. "Therefore, my beloved brethren whom I long to see, my joy and my crown, so stand firm (stay) in the Lord, my beloved" (Philippians 4:1). The problem comes when we disregard these commands. Like the puppy in obedience class, our attention span is very short. If we feel like Jesus gave these commands but is now somewhere behind a closed door, we begin to feel it is acceptable to ignore the commands. Within a short time, we are completely disregarding God's Word, and therefore, our relationship with Christ. Paul understood this temptation. "For you were called to freedom, brethren; only do not turn your freedom into an opportunity for the flesh, but through love serve one another" (Galatians 5:13). Peter agreed, "Act as free men, and do not use your freedom as a covering for evil, but use it as bondslaves of God" (1 Peter 2:16).

The great thing about working with dogs is that they can change. Patterns can be broken quickly when we change our expectations and energy. If your dog does not stay, then start over. Teach them again, and this time, expect them to follow your direction by projecting that energy to the dog. An old dog *can* learn new tricks.

The same is true with us. We may have disregarded the commands of Jesus and strayed from our knowledge of him. There may be sin and guilt that is blocking us, leaving us feeling as though he could not possibly forgive us. What is true for our dogs is also true for us. Our hearts can change as our faithful obedience changes. The following passage is for us:

> "Now to Him who is able to keep you from stumbling, and to make you stand in the presence of His glory blameless with great joy, to the only God our Savior, through Jesus Christ our Lord, be glory, majesty, dominion and authority, before all time and now and forever. Amen."
>
> Jude 24–25

Have you ever seen a nervous dog that tries to follow the master's command but dances nervously, shakes, and twitches? They want to trust, but their apprehension blocks them from enjoying a submissive relationship with their master. We often act like those dogs. We hear a sermon, read a passage, understand a new concept, and agree with it. Yet our spirit is dancing nervously, fearing that we can never enjoy the promises.

Our youth group had learned how to lead others through the "Four Spiritual Laws" pamphlet. It seemed only natural that they should practice on real people. So we loaded the group into a bus and headed for the city park. I was excited about the prospects. The kids were petrified! They knew that they loved God, and they genuinely wanted to trust me, but their apprehension was a huge problem. When we arrived at the park,

I sent them out in teams of two while I positioned myself in a location where I could see them at all times. Teams avoided people at first, dancing around them nervously. After a while they cautiously approached random people who looked safe. At one point, one of the boys came running toward me with a panicked look on his face. When he reached me, he was out of breath but managed to speak in broken phrases. "I need... your help. I... met a lady... and she wants to know about Jesus... What do I do?"

Together we returned to the tennis courts where the two had met, and I supported him as he shared the gospel with her. To his amazement, and I must admit mine as well, she accepted Jesus right there in the park. The following Sunday she came to church and became a vital part of our congregation.

If you have ever felt like the boy in my youth group, then the Apostle Peter has some important words for you.

> "And who is there to harm you if you prove zealous for what is good? But even if you should suffer for the sake of righteousness, you are blessed. And do not fear their intimidation and do not be troubled, but sanctify Christ as Lord in your hearts, always being ready to make a defense to everyone who asks you to give an account for the hope that is in you, yet with gentleness and reverence; and keep a good conscience so that in the thing in which you are slandered, those who revile your good behavior in Christ may be put to shame."
>
> 1 Peter 3:13–16

God wants to build, or rebuild, his relationship with you. The peace of Christ is yours. Freedom from fear is yours. A close, loving relationship with the Lord is yours. Your job is to stay in him, his Word, and his love. Practice every day, and allow God to bless you. You will discover quickly that the apprehension is gone, and your ability to stay will become easier as you grow in Christ.

> "Now to Him who is able to do exceedingly abundantly beyond all that we ask or think, according to the power that works within us, to Him be the glory in the church and in Christ Jesus to all generations forever and ever."
>
> Ephesians 3:20–21

Think It Through

Passages used to illustrate "Stay": Psalm 23; John 8:31–32; John 15:7; John 15:9–10; Philippians 4:1; Galatians 5:13; 1 Peter 2:16; Jude 24–25; 1 Peter 3:13–16; Ephesians 3:20–21.

On Your Own

Our dogs react to certain triggers that affect their behavior. It may be a scent, a sight, or even a sound that sends them over the edge. We can detect the difference in our pets because they become tense, begin to shake, or pace. We have triggers as well. A sweet smell may remind us of holidays spent in the kitchen with family. This is a trigger. Sights and sounds can even be our trigger. We may not react immediately to the trigger, but we feel the reaction. Make a list of your triggers. Identify those things that cause you stress. Write them down before moving on.

_____

_____

_____

In the dog world, we have the power to redirect energy. We may do this through the leash, with a word, or with a touch. It does not require a dramatic move on our part. We simply need to change their focus away from the trigger and onto our leadership. Go through your list of triggers and identify ways that you can redirect your own energy, or you can ask for help to redirect. Take those ideas and ask someone to become your accountability partner. We will not learn to stay unless we create the mechanism that will keep us on track.

_____

_____

_____

Read Romans 10:8–11. Use the list you created, along with your ideas to redirect your energy, and pray through them. Find a place to be alone with God and pray out loud. Confess with your mouth and let the words be heard by your own ears. Pray for forgiveness and ask for God's help. Pray that he may redirect you and bring you peace.

SECTION THREE
Learning from the Pack

Pulling As a Team

Kim and I have a regular route to our walks. From our porch, around the loop, and back to our porch is exactly one mile. We do have alternate routes that range anywhere from a half mile to two and a half miles. However, our usual walk follows the same one-mile path. The last few months have been particularly interesting, since we have been walking Jazzy, Satchmo, and the puppies.

Recently, as we walked down the street, our pack met three little girls, busily decorating the sidewalk with chalk. One of them looked up from her artwork and said, "Oh, look. It's the cute puppies." After a few minutes of tail wagging and giggling, we were back on course. As we walked away, I was struck by the visible impact that two people and their pack of dogs can have. Individually, we draw very little attention. But together, everybody notices us.

God never intended for us to experience our faith in a vacuum. He did not ask us to stand alone. In fact, the opposite is true. He makes us a part of his pack, the church.

Within the church, God has provided other believers who stand beside us, support us, protect us, and cause us to grow in our relationship with Jesus. The church allows us to have a presence in our community, our country, and around the globe. Alone, we would draw little attention, but together we can change the world.

The Power of the Pack

After Tippy (the first dog I remember) died of old age, my parents decided that they did not want to have another dog. They were convinced that they could not replace Tippy, and they weren't interested in trying. For some reason, I decided that we needed to have another canine companion. In typical childhood fashion, I begged, whined, cried, and refused to accept no for an answer. At one point, I retrieved Tippy's leash from the kitchen junk drawer and carried it around wherever I went. Finally, my father gave in, vowing that the dog would be mine, and that his total care was up to me. (If you are a parent, you know where this is going.)

The dog I chose came from the local animal shelter. The name Poncho was written on the front of the kennel. He was a terrier mix with the body of a bull terrier. He was a high-energy dog, while I was a low-energy master. The results of our relationship were less than satisfactory. I did not provide leadership for him, so he did everything he could to control me. I did not walk him because he was too strong. When I did take him out, he became so excited that he would knock me down and drag me around. He was lonely and anxious, but I did not understand how to interpret his behavior. What he wanted was leadership, and what he got was a master who ignored him. Ultimately, I did what most kids do with pets. I left him to my parents (you knew that would happen). I still have a vivid picture in my mind of Poncho sitting on the roof of his doghouse, watching the back door, hoping that I would come outside and offer the love and attention that he needed.

A happy dog needs leadership and companionship. He needs other dogs to learn from. He needs the energy that comes from being a part of a group. A happy dog must have the chance to exercise his breed instincts. He must be able to use his energy in positive and constructive ways. Dogs want to be happy and healthy, and they need us to help them achieve a balanced state of energy. Without our help, dogs become nervous, difficult to manage, and even neurotic. Fortunately for Poncho, my father was good with animals. Once it was clear that I had a lot to learn about animals, he stepped in and began to shape Poncho into a very good dog.

What is true for dogs is also true for people. Christians need fellowship and the support of others to grow. Being around fellow Christians helps us to achieve a balanced faith, allows us feel comfortable as a part of a group, and gives us an opportunity to exercise our gifts. From its inception, God intended for us to have support from other believers. He created the church, his body, and made us a part of it, so we could grow into mature, well-balanced Christians. We see in Acts 2 that people quickly embraced this concept.

> "So then, those who had received his word were baptized; and there were added that day about three thousand souls. And they were continually devoting themselves to the apostles teaching and to fellowship, to the breaking of bread and to prayer. And everyone kept feeling a sense of awe; and many wonders and signs were taking place through the apostles. And all those who had believed were together, and had all things in common."
>
> Acts 2:41–44

"Not one of them claimed that anything belonging to him was his own; but all things were common property" (Acts 4:32). "And also the people from the cities in the vicinity of Jerusalem were coming together" (Acts 5:16). "And the word of God kept on spreading; and the number of disciples continued to increase greatly in Jerusalem" (Acts 6:7).

The early church was dynamic. It was alive and

vibrant. People were drawn to it. They learned about Christ. They learned how to become like Christ. They heard it in words, but they observed it in the lives of those around them. The church became an essential part of their lives.

The church has not changed, nor has the truth of the Gospel. The same power, wisdom, and strength can be found in the fellowship of believers today. It is the place where the truth of Scripture meets today's issues. You need the body of Christ, and the body of Christ needs you.

> "The end of all things is at hand; therefore, be of sound judgment and sober spirit for the purpose of prayer. Above all, keep fervent in your love for one another, because love covers a multitude of sins. Be hospitable to one another without complaint. As each one has received a special gift, employ it in serving one another, as good stewards of the manifold grace of God."
>
> 1 Peter 4:7–10

Several months ago, our granddaughter Elyse accompanied us on one of our evening walks. As we passed by one of the homes on our route, a large black Labrador began to bark frantically through the iron back yard fence. Our granddaughter was startled by the size of the animal and the ferocious sound of its bark. As we passed the house, the dog ran around behind the back of the house to the iron gate on the other side. As soon as we came into view, he started barking once again. This time, Elyse was unnerved. Our own dogs picked up on her fear and began to respond with barks of their own.

Since my early struggles with Poncho, I have learned to listen much more carefully to animals. I pay more attention to a dog's voice and observe their movements. The dog behind the iron gate wasn't angry. He was lonely. So, in full view of the barking dog, I leaned over to reassure my granddaughter. In a calm voice, I informed her that the dog she feared was not angry at all. Nor did he want to hurt us. He was barking because he wanted to come on a walk with us. I encouraged her to listen to his voice, to see if she could hear him say, "Please, take me. I want to go on the walk with you."

Elyse listened with new understanding, and her fear turned to compassion for the lonely dog. Amazingly, the dog sensed her change in attitude because his tail began wagging feverishly, and he literally began to bounce with excitement. As we continued on our walk, Elyse listened for other lonely dogs that wanted to come on a walk with us. She heard a lot of lonely voices.

Recently, while out on another walk with our pack, the Labrador saw us coming. He ran around his house with familiar regularity. This time, however, when he hit the iron gate it swung wide open. Free from his bonds, he rushed toward us. Was I right about his loneliness? It was time to find out. We stopped and allowed his approach. He showed all of the subtle signs of submission. His tail was flat with his body, head down, and his ears were relaxed. Once he reached us, you could hear his heavy sigh of relief. He was finally meeting the pack that he longed to walk with. He was calm, and our dogs were happy with his presence.

Our world is full of lonely voices. They are the voices of people who are isolated in their jobs, neighborhoods, and communities. They rush to work, sit in cubicles, and fight one another to get home so they can lock themselves in their houses to rest up to do it again. They are lonely to walk with others who are like them. They need fellowship, others to walk with, to gain strength from, and to learn from. This is what the church is all about. If you are a vital part of your church, you understand this point well. There is tremendous power in walking with God's pack, exercising your gifts and abilities in his service.

Listen to the barks of the people around you. They raise all sorts of questions, objections, and excuses about why they don't need a church. But if you listen to their voices beyond the words they speak and listen with compassion, you will begin to hear their plea. "Rescue me from my isolation, and let me go on this walk with you."

Think It Through

Passages used to illustrate "The Power of the Pack": Acts 2:41–44; Acts 4:32; Acts 5:16; Acts 6:7; 1 Peter 4:7–10.

The Support of the Pack

God has made every believer a part of his pack, the church. "For just as we have many members in one body, and all the members do not have the same function, so we, who are many members, are one body and individually members of one another" (Romans 12:4–5). This church, of which God has made you a part, is a vital ingredient to your spiritual growth.

> "Let us hold fast the confession of our hope without wavering, for He who promises is faithful; and let us consider how to stimulate one another to love and good deeds, not forsaking our own assembling

together, as is the habit of some, but encouraging one another, and all the more as you see the day draw near."

Hebrews 10:23–25

While taking a group of students to a marine biology camp on Catalina Island in California, I learned a great lesson that amplified this passage. The group was kayaking along the shoreline, near Two Harbors, when we found ourselves surrounded by a kelp bed. Our instructor used the opportunity to teach us about kelp. Kelp grows in thick beds, where each stock protects the other stalks from the turbulence of the waves. It can do all of this because at the bottom of each plant is a thick root system that attaches itself onto the rocks on the ocean floor. That root system is called a "hold fast." The health of a kelp bed is dependent upon its ability to hold fast to the rocks below. Likewise, the health of the church is equally dependant upon our ability to hold fast to the rock of our salvation, Jesus Christ. When we are a part of a church, we find the same level of strength and support that is found in a kelp bed.

It is so important that we have a church to stand by us when we struggle or become weak. It is the one place where we can go to find people of like mind who can build us up and help us grow in Christ. "For you were called to freedom, brethren; only do not turn your freedom into an opportunity for the flesh, but through love, serve one another" (Galatians 5:13). "Bear one another's burdens, and thus fulfill the law of Christ" (Galatians 6:2).

In January of 2006, a group of faithful people believed that God wanted to begin a ministry to single adults in our church. They approached me to work with them and become their leader. Their vision for what God could do in people's lives was inspiring, and I joyfully agreed to become a part of that ministry. On our first Sunday, two months later, 113 people came together to learn more about Jesus. Since its inception, God has touched many lives with renewed hope and spiritual strength. It has been such a joy to watch hurting people come into our group and become whole again. By coming, they found people with common needs and interests and felt comfortable opening their lives to one another. Their desire to love and serve one another has caused this ministry to develop into a dynamic organism within the church. They believed the words of 1 John 1:7, "If we walk in the light as He Himself is in the light, we have fellowship with one another, and the blood of Jesus His Son cleanses us from all sin."

Being part of God's pack, the church, also allows us to share our common faith in corporate worship. Paul wrote,

> "So then do not be foolish, but understand what the will of the Lord is. And do not get drunk with wine, for this is dissipation, but be filled with the Spirit speaking to one another in psalms and hymns and spiritual songs, singing and making melody with your heart to the Lord."
>
> Ephesians 5:17–19

When we come together as the body of Christ, we open the Word of God, apply its content to our lives, sing songs of faith, and support one another so that we can follow in the footsteps of Jesus.

In his book, *Be the Pack Leader,* Cesar Millan reminds us that we must fulfill the breed instincts of our dog. Herding dogs need to herd something in order to feel balanced. Hounds need to track, while retrievers need to practice retrieving. Terriers need to dig, to go into holes, and root out vermin. When they operate within their breed strengths, they can be amazing.

But think about this from the other side for a minute. You cannot expect a Great Dane to enter a small hole and root out a gopher, or a basset hound to herd cattle. They can try, but they will be working against their strengths.

I once traveled with a friend to Round Valley, Idaho, where his family owned a cattle ranch. The purpose of our trip was to collect firewood off the property. We traveled nearly a mile from the house to a corner of the ranch, where we spent the day cutting standing dead trees. Kevin had a Labrador retriever who loved to play fetch. The whole time that we worked, my friend was throwing a pinecone, which his dog would chase down, bring back, and lie at his master's feet. After a few hours, my friend grew weary of the game. At a time when the dog was not watching, Kevin dropped the pinecone down a hole made by a ground squirrel. The lab busied himself with the task of looking for the pinecone, but it was nowhere to be found. Finally, he settled down for a nap in the back of the truck.

At the end of the day, with a truck full of wood, we headed back to the ranch house and prepared for a restful night. About two o'clock in the morning, the dog started barking. He danced, dug at the door, and barked furiously. Thinking that an animal had wandered too near the house, my friend opened the door and let his dog out. The Lab leapt off of the porch and disappeared from sight. With silence regained, we settled back down to continue our much-needed rest. We were surprised the next morning to find the lab sleeping on the front porch, covered in dirt, with the very same pinecone lying under his chin. In the middle of the night, he had figured it out, ran back to that spot, dug a huge hole, and retrieved his pinecone. He was doing what he was bred to do. God has designed us with natural abilities. When we use them, we find fulfillment and happiness. He has also given each of us a spiritual gift:

> "For the equipping of the saints for the work of service, to the building up of the body of Christ; until we all attain to the unity of the faith, and of the knowledge of the Son of God, to a mature man, to the measure of the stature which belongs to the fullness of Christ."
>
> Ephesians 4:12–13

If we want to be well-balanced, mature Christians, then we need to use both gifts and talents in ministry.

You may be confused at this point, questioning your value in the church. Is there a gift that God has granted to you? Is there a ministry that he has called you to fulfill? The Scriptures answer to both questions is yes. You may need to think it through and do some digging in your own life, but God will help you figure it out.

I have been around the church all of my life, involved in some sort of ministry for most of those years. I have heard the horror stories of those who were alienated by the church, hurt by fellow Christians, or worked to the point of exhaustion. The church roles are filled with names of people who no longer attend. You may be one of those people. I have had negative experiences of my own. It is easy to harbor negative feelings from past hurts. Yet within the context of this book, let me encourage you. Live in the moment. Like the canine that you love, change your approach, and your attitude will follow. Others may have betrayed your trust, but now God wants to bring people into your life to begin the healing process. Live in the moment.

Think It Through

Passages used to illustrate "The Support of the Pack": Romans 12:4–5; Hebrews 10:23–25; Galatians 5:13; Galatians 6:2; 1 John 1:7; Ephesians 5:17–19; Ephesians 4:12–13.

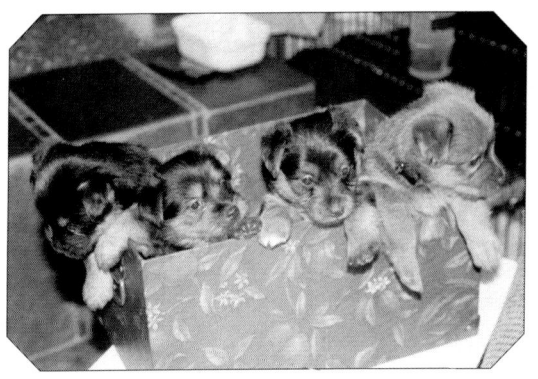

The Hope of the Pack

"Let not your heart be troubled, believe in God, believe also in Me. In My Father's house are many dwelling places; if it were not so, I would have told you; for I go to prepare a place for you. And if I go and prepare a place for you, I will come again, and receive you to Myself; that where I am, there you may be also."

John 14:1–3

This statement from our Lord is what sets the church apart from any other organization on earth. What the church does has everlasting results. We have the hope of a heavenly home with Jesus.

About this hope of glory, Paul wrote,

> "Behold, I tell you a mystery, we shall not all sleep, but we shall all be changed, in a moment, in the twinkling of an eye, at the last trumpet; for the trumpet will sound, and the dead will be raised imperishable, and we shall be changed. For the perishable must put on the imperishable, and this mortal must put on immortality. But when this perishable will have put on the imperishable, and this mortal will have put on immortality, then will come about the saying that is written, 'Death is swallowed up in victory. O death, where is your victory? O death, where is your sting? The sting of death is sin, and the power of sin is the law; but thanks be to God, who gives us the victory through our Lord Jesus Christ.'"
> 1 Corinthians 15:51–57

I must say that most of the time people talk about the second coming, they quote these verses, and they usually stop at verse 57 like we did here. However, there is one more verse to this important text. It is one that we must not ignore, since it includes our marching orders that lead up to the second coming. Verse 58 says, "Therefore, my beloved brethren, be steadfast, immovable, always abounding in the work of the Lord, knowing that your toil is not in vain in the Lord."

To be steadfast is to be firmly placed in a single location. So Paul tells us that those who will be raised with Christ are those who are secure in their relationship with Christ, immovable in their confident faith, and active in the Lord's service. This is a tall order that cannot be fulfilled on our own floating in the waves of the world. We must be around others of like faith, protecting them, being protected by their fellowship, and holding fast to Jesus Christ, the rock of our salvation.

God wants to have a very special relationship with us. As the leader of the pack, He calls us to surrender to him, to assume the down position, and to settle in his presence. He calls us to discipleship, urging us to sit, calling us to "leave it" when we stray from his path, and offering all his blessings with "take it." He desires to live by acts of faith. When he says, "come," we come. When he says, "wait," we trust his timing, and when he tells us to "stay," we accept his judgment. We are steadfast, immovable, and committed to his ministry.

When we do these things, then like Paul, we will be able to say,

> "I have fought the good fight, I have finished the course, I have kept the faith; in the future there is laid up for me the crown of righteousness, which the Lord, the righteous Judge, will award to me on that day; and not only to me, but also to all who have loved His appearing."
>
> 2 Timothy 4:7–8

Think It Through

Passages used to illustrate "The Hope of the Pack": John 14:1–3; 1 Corinthians 15:51–58; 2 Timothy 4:7–8.

On Your Own

Read 1 Corinthians 12:20–31. What does it say about the church and your role in the body of Christ? Can someone honestly say, "I don't need to be involved in ministry?" Can we proclaim others as important while believing that it doesn't matter if we are involved or not?

Many people shun the church in order to justify themselves for not being involved. Read Romans 12:9–21. What is God saying to you about his church?

According to this passage, how can you change your approach to the church so that you can get the most out of your relationship with the Lord?

Photo courtesy of Westminster Kennel Club

Epilogue: Old Dog, New Tricks; It's Never Too Late

The Westminster Kennel Club Dog Show is the most prestigious dog show in America. In fact, the Westminster Dog Show is the second oldest sporting event of any kind in the United States, at 133 years and counting. The competition brings champion dogs from all over the country to compete for the "Best in Show" title. The top competitors are by invitation only, with less than half of the other competitors filled by applicants. When you show at Westminster, you are thought to have arrived in the dog show world. The 2009 winner broke from tradition by crowning a ten-year-old Sussex Spaniel as the "Best In Show."

Stump, whose American Kennel Club registered name is Ch. Clussexx Three D Grinchy Glee, is the oldest champion in the history of the competition. He is not a novice to winning competitions, though, having won more than fifty "Best in Show" titles. What makes him unique is the rest of his story.

Stump was forced into retirement in 2005 due to a serious illness. At one point, Stump was in an animal hospital, near death. His vital organs had shut down, and the doctors had no idea why. With no understanding of what was wrong, they could only treat him through trial and error. It was only through an educated guess that they found a medication that would work for him. Even with that, his recovery was slow.

Stump's owners had not entered him in any competition since that illness. Early in the week, prior to Westminster, they still had no idea that Stump would compete. It was almost like Stump knew that the competition was about to happen, because he seemed to rise to his former glory. At the last minute, they decided to take Stump to New York.

On the opening day of the competition, Stump topped all other Sussex spaniels in his class, taking "Best of Breed." Then he was named top in the sporting group against pointers, setters, spaniels, and retrievers. This is a tough group with well-known and popular breeds. When Stump entered the "Best in Show" ring, the crowd took notice of him. He quickly became a crowd favorite, and they began cheering for him. The judge had no idea of Stump's age, of his retirement, or his medical history. She saw a dog, which, on that day, perfectly exemplified what a Sussex spaniel should look like. After marking her scores in the register, she pointed to Stump and named him the winner. After a five-year retirement and a near-death experience, he was "Best in Show," the oldest winner in history, and the first Sussex spaniel to wear the title.

Perhaps you have heard it said that old dogs don't learn new tricks. If you hear it enough times, you start to believe the statement to be fact. Yet the truth is, dogs can learn new things at any age. They can also change their behavior to be restored to the good behaviors of the past. There is no time stamp on a dog's ability to change.

What is true in the animal world is also true in our Christian faith. It is never too late for you to be restored and renewed by the loving forgiveness of Jesus Christ. There is no time limit on grace, and no expiration date on God's forgiveness. You can be changed. You can be transformed. You can be raised from the dead.

While today's problem may seem insurmountable at times, we need to remember the promise of God offered long ago. "Be strong and courageous, do not be afraid or tremble at them, for the Lord your God is the one who goes with you. He will not fail you nor forsake you" (Deuteronomy 31:6). You are not bound by the pain of the past. You can begin to correct behaviors immediately. Stop replaying the old events in your mind. You can forge a new path and create a new reality.

It is possible that you have read through this book, enjoyed the stories, and completed the assignments at the end of each chapter, yet an old burden still presses hard on you. It is time for you to taste the sweet forgiveness of the Lord Jesus Christ.

The good news of the gospel is that it is never too late for you to be restored. You can be renewed by the loving forgiveness of Jesus Christ. There is no time limit on grace and no expiration date on God's forgiveness. You can be changed. You can be transformed. You can be raised from the dead.

Before you go down the all-too-familiar path of saying that Jesus can't possibly forgive what you have done, let's look briefly at the people Jesus has already forgiven. Jesus offered forgiveness to a prostitute, to a tax swindler, and to a man who was full of demons. He accepted doubters, outcasts, and people who were rejected by society. He forgave those who hated him and those who sentenced him to death. He forgave those who beat him. He even offered a place in paradise to a criminal who was crucified next to him. He offered love and forgiveness to those who denied him.

At one point in his ministry, this comment was recorded: "Now all the tax-gatherers and the sinners were coming near Him to listen to Him. And both the Pharisees and the scribes began to grumble, saying, 'This man receives sinners and eats with them'" (Luke 15:1–2). Jesus' response is important in this discussion.

"But when He heard this, He said, 'It is not those who are healthy who need a physician, but those who are sick'" (Matthew 9:12).

Jesus transformed the life of Paul, known at the time as Saul, who went about leading those who wanted to murder believers. I am certain that none of these people were newcomers to a life of sin. They were dead in their sin, as lost as any before them and any after them. They were dead, but Jesus set them free and made them champions. The Apostle Paul proclaimed,

> "Therefore let it be known to you, brethren, that through Him forgiveness of sin is proclaimed to you, and through Him everyone who believes is freed from all things, from which you could not be freed through the Law of Moses."
>
> Acts 13:38–39

If running from the issues you face solves them, then by all means, put on your track shoes. Put as much distance as you can between yourself and the sin that brings you pain. But if the problem does not go away and it threatens your spiritual life, then another tactic is required. When you cannot go over them, under them, or around your issues, then the only way to find freedom is to go through them. If you are ready to walk through "the valley of the shadow of death," then understand this; you are not going into that valley alone. To those who have already walked this path, God offers this reminder:

> "And you were dead in your trespasses and sins. In which you formerly walked according to the course of this world, according to the prince of the power

of the air, of the spirit that is now working in the sons of disobedience. Among them we too all formerly lived in the lusts of the flesh, indulging the desires of the flesh and of the mind, and were by nature children of wrath, even as the rest. But God, being rich in mercy, because of His great love with which He loved us, even when we were dead in our transgression, made us alive together with Christ (by grace you have been saved), and raised us up with Him, and seated us with Him in the heavenly places in Christ Jesus."

Ephesians 2:1–6

To those who are too weak to deal with their sin alone, the Apostle Paul gives this testimony: "And He has said to me, 'My grace is sufficient for you, for power is perfected in weakness.' Most gladly, therefore, I will rather boast about my weaknesses, that the power of Christ may dwell in me" (2 Corinthians 12:9). Paul understood the weight of sin and knew the way to reverse its effects. He followed Jesus' call to "take my yoke."

When we are strong, we have no idea how much weight Jesus is carrying on our behalf. But when we are weak, his power and provisions become obvious. The weight would crush us if Jesus were not carrying the yoke with us.

"If we confess our sins, He is faithful and righteous to forgive us our sins and to cleanse us from all unrighteousness" (1 John 1:9). What I have learned in my own life is that it is much easier to discuss my sin with someone who has had similar experiences and found freedom. They will understand, and become a support to help me break the chains and find the times of refreshment that is promised in Scripture. Many churches offer support groups, like AA or Celebrate Recovery, that are dedicated to helping people work through the traps they have fallen into.

There are grief groups, singles groups, and many different types of support programs available if you seek them out. Pastors are more than anxious to help reverse the effects of the weight that is on you. They are knowledgeable in the Scriptures and will do their best to counsel you and pray with you. Pastors can put you in touch with whatever support group you need, even if that group meets at a different church. There is nothing more important to God, and therefore to the church, than for you to find the forgiveness that Christ died to give you.

> "For the grace of God has appeared, bringing salvation to all men, instructing us to deny ungodliness and worldly desires and to live sensibly, righteously and godly in the present age, looking for the blessed hope and the appearing of the glory of our great God and Savior, Christ Jesus; who gave Himself for us, that He might redeem us from every lawless deed and purify for Himself a people for His own possession, zealous for good deeds."
> Titus 2:11–14

Don't let this weight crush you. Stop beating yourself over the head. Make this the day that you have a resurrection of heart and mind. It is never too late. You are never too far gone to be restored by the grace of Jesus. Give yourself completely to the One who would be your pack leader, and follow his commands of surrender, obedience, and faithfulness. Allow the pack to support you, so you can experience the joy of the Lord. If another step is required to gain freedom, do not let this day go by without locating a support group. A happy, well-balanced Christian life awaits you.

> "And who is there to harm you if you prove zealous for what is good? But even if you should suffer for the sake of righteousness, you are blessed. And do not fear their intimidation, and do not be troubled, but sanctify Christ as Lord in your hearts, always being ready to make a defense to everyone who asks you to give an account for the hope that is in you, yet with gentleness and reverence; and keep a good conscience so that in the thing in which you are slandered, those who revile your good behavior in Christ may be put to shame. For it is better, if God should will it so, that you suffer for doing what is right rather than for doing what is wrong."
> 1 Peter 3:13–17

Heavenly Father, I lift up the reader of this book and ask that you draw near to them. Bring conviction to areas of their life where you have been shut out. Anoint the areas where new growth is taking place. Give a newfound sense of joy as they grow in understanding of what it means to be a disciple. May the simplicity of this book draw believers into the depths of your love. In Jesus' name, amen.

Bibliography

The New American Standard Bible. The Lockman Foundation, La Habra, California. Holman Bible Publishers, Nashville, Tennessee, 1960.

Cesar's Way. Cesar, Millan, Melissa Jo Peltier. Three Rivers Press, New York, New York, 2006.

Be the Pack Leader. Cesar Millan, Melissa Jo Peltier. Three Rivers Press, New York, New York, 2007.